How to Run a Successful Market Stall

A Simple Guide for
Food Producers and Crafters

Library and Archives Canada Cataloguing in Publication

Zaruba, Dana
How to run a successful market stall : a simple guide for food producers and crafters / Dana Zaruba.

Includes bibliographical references.
Issued also in electronic format.

ISBN 978-0-9867824-0-4

1. Street vendors. 2. Vending stands. 3. Markets. 4. New business

enterprises--Management. 5. Success in business. I. Title.

HF5470.Z37 2011   381'.18 C2010-907989-2

Edited by Betty Taylor
Book Design by Linda Parke   www.lindaparke.com
Photography by Sarah Hall and by the author

Printed in the United States of America

Published by
Over Unity Press,
P. O. Box 332 Cobble Hill, BC
V0R 1L0

www.overunitypress.com

To my parents, Olga and Jerry Zaruba for encouraging me to blossom as an artist and free spirit while reminding me that I still need to keep my feet firmly planted in the practical aspects of life. You both continue to be an inspiration in my life.

To Paul, Linda, Lulu, Monica, Heather and especially Rob, for all your Love, support and steadfast belief that what I have to share is of value to others. You see through the shell to the essence.

Finally, to all of my customers and fellow vendors whose feedback and suggestions have helped shape the direction of my business and life.

Thank you, Thank you, *Thank* you.

Dana

Table of Contents

Introduction

My journey through the world of selling at markets started in 2000 when I created my first nut and spice blend. I knew virtually nothing about running a market stall and learned mostly through trial and error. I looked in bookstores and the library for a book on how to run a market stall but really couldn't find one that covered all the details. I learned more from pestering a lot of friendly vendors with myriad questions. With a decade of experience now under my belt, I have enjoyed helping new vendors with many of the same questions I had when I first started. I realized, though, that it would be more helpful if I just wrote all the tips I share into a useful little guide. This book is the result. No matter what your product is, following the suggestions in this book will help you create a more successful market stall than if you simply "winged it."

Being successful means different things to different people. Contrary to most corporate policy success is often *not* about making the most profit. For many, selling at the markets is more about being active in the community or as a way of funding a hobby. For others, it is a way of introducing their arts and crafts to the public, or selling excess produce they grew in their gardens. For some, it is a social calling to educate and help inform the public about our changing world and our responsibility to heal and nurture our planet. Whatever your goals, this book will help you along that path.

While it is still rare, there are some vendors, myself included, for whom a market business is their only source of revenue. Given today's difficult economic times, many vendors are relying increasingly on market revenue as an important additional income source to support their families. Our world is changing and so are our priorities. What might have been a fun hobby for some may start to transform into a necessary income. With that often comes confusion as to how to start or develop one's market business into a more viable income.

My intention is to help you develop an efficient, profitable and sustainable market business, whatever your product or goals. It is my sincerest wish to be of service and if just one person reading this book is inspired to go forward with their own market business, or improve the one they've already started, then I will be grateful for the chance to be part of that process.

THE OBJECTIVES OF THIS BOOK

Running a successful market stand usually requires more preparation than putting a few products onto a bare table and then sitting in a chair waiting for customers to buy them. Simple but effective planning can greatly increase your chances of success and elevate the enjoyment for all.

This book has been written to help you:

- Choose the best possible products to sell at today's marketplace.

- Set up your business effectively and with the least amount of difficulty.

- Make and display your products to attract customers.

- Cost and price your products, and learn effective sales techniques.

- Manage your market day efficiently.

- Deal with difficult situations, and navigate market politics.

Helping you succeed benefits the other vendors as well as the customers. With just a little focused effort, you can bring excellence, self-sufficiency, prosperity and pride to yourself and your community. Others will become inspired by your good example and the desire to improve will increase the quality and viability of the entire market.

Only you can define what success means to you, but if you are going to sell at market, taking some thoughtful and simple steps to become organized and efficient will make the experience more enjoyable and profitable.

Getting Started

*I*t is a good idea to know what you'll need to do before you get into markets so you are as well prepared as you can be prior to going to your first market day. If you follow the list below, you'll be ready! All of these things will be covered in detail in subsequent chapters.

Do some research on each kind of market and decide what to sell.

Find production space, suppliers and get your business set up.

Get any necessary health forms, licenses, permits and insurance.

Make, bake or grow your product and calculate your costs and prices.

Apply to the markets.

Get your market tent, table, display, signage, display units, and supplies.

Set up your market tent and display at home prior to going to your first market.

Head to the market, and sell, sell, sell!

Review the events of your market day, and do your banking.

TYPES OF MARKETS

Markets can be exciting and vibrant places, each with its own unique set of qualities and idiosyncrasies. One of the most frequent questions I get asked is: *"Which are the good markets to go to?"* To answer that, I've compiled a list of the different kinds of markets to help you choose what kind of market would best suit your products.

There are increasing numbers of great markets available for you to attend, but how do you go about finding them all? You can visit www.farmersmarketscanada.ca for links to provincial market associations that will have lists of the markets in your area, click on *American Sites of Interest*, and check under resources for a list of state market associations. Click on the site map, scroll down a bit and look up www.farmersmarketcoalition.org/

A tip for navigating through extensive websites is to click on their **site map**, which lists all the pages on their website in a simple format, making it much easier to find the information you need.

FARMERS' MARKETS

When one thinks of the words, "farmers' market," it conjures up the idea of farming families selling food they produced on their own family farms. This is traditionally what a farmers' market is supposed to represent. They are usually held once a week and set up in an open field, parking lot or down a street. While some markets are housed in permanent, covered structures, many are simply set up in temporary spaces outside and run rain or shine. Produce, eggs, meats, cheeses, breads, seafood and preserves are sold directly by the producer.

Some farmers' markets do allow vendors to come from farther away and even allow the resale of foods purchased from wholesale or import brokers.

Thoroughly review your market's policies or you may find yourself having difficulty competing with these resale vendors. Fortunately for local producers, many farmers' markets have strict policies against the resale of wholesale produce, but as with anything, this has its advantages and disadvantages.

ADVANTAGES

- Strictly producer-run markets have little to no competition from imports or wholesale sellers

- Loyal customers whose main reason for coming to market is to buy local foods from you, the local friendly farmer

- Busy, vibrant atmosphere, great community feeling

- Retail markup means more profit in your pocket

- Good for a family business. Some allow you to bring your children to the market.

DISADVANTAGES

- If you do not have a greenhouse, you may not be able to sell anything before late spring or summer. If your market does not allow for resale, you can only sell what you grow, raise or harvest yourself. This can limit your market season.

- You will likely need a second or third income if yours is not a large operation. Most families today cannot live only on farmers' market revenue.

- If the weather does not cooperate you may have fewer products to offer.

- You might have a large initial and ongoing outlay of money for farming and food production infrastructure.

- You may not qualify for government support or grants if your operation is too small or you do not grow commodity crops like soy or corn.

- Getting organic certification can be a long, difficult and expensive process. While there are certainly moral and health benefits of going organic, the economic benefits might not be available to you.

- If you are a craft vendor, food-only farmers' markets might exclude you from attending, or they might have a limit on the percentage of craft vendors allowed to attend.

CRAFT MARKETS

These are markets where one can finds jewelry, cloth goods, wooden toys, furniture, decorative objects, cards, artwork, garden art, and sometimes snack or candy vendors, kettle corn, and chocolates, with various food carts selling coffees, hotdogs, fried donuts and ice cream.

ADVANTAGES

- People going to craft markets are craft lovers, so you've already got an interested audience.

- There will be few if any produce vendors as competition.

- Depending on the level and expertise of those judging for craft quality and uniqueness, there can be exceptional quality available for sale.

- If you are looking to enter the arts and crafts world, markets can be an excellent way to assess the public's reception of your work.

- You may not view markets as a business, but rather as a way of reaching out to others if you are going through life changing times. Creating and selling crafts can be a way for you to stretch your wings and show people who you are, or maybe, who you'd like to be. Markets can provide a safe public venue that allows for this kind of self-exploration.

- Successfully selling your work can be artistically validating and can lead to invitations to gallery shows, special events, private commissions and even teaching opportunities.

- You have an advantage over large corporations in your ability to quickly adopt or create a trend to fill niche markets. Large corporations simply cannot adapt to regional trends as quickly or efficiently as you can.

DISADVANTAGES

- Many customers go to craft markets just for something to do when relatives are in town, and may not be interested in buying. As a result, you really have to hone your selling techniques.

- Selling your crafts can be challenging during difficult economic times when the public is focused on paying for essentials. This is why it is even more crucial to make the most beautiful, skilled crafts you can. Why bother making a mediocre product that can be purchased for a fraction of the cost at a large box store. In tough economic times, it is even more important to add value to your creations by making them very special, unique and versatile.

- If rejection is difficult for you or you are exceptionally shy, failure to sell your products can also be very hard on your self-esteem.

- If the market organizers haven't chosen a wide range of products, competition may be fierce. This often happens with jewelry vendors. There may be just too much of one type of craft available.

- Vendors' product quality and uniqueness may be limited in some markets, creating inconsistencies, confusion for the public and a general lack of cohesiveness in the feeling of the market.

FLEA MARKETS

Flea markets are venues where people sell items similar to what they'd sell at a garage sale. Bargaining is common.

ADVANTAGES

- If you refurbish items bought from flea markets, or have items made from vintage materials, you might just find a niche market.

- If you sell typical market foods like kettle corn, candy floss or have a catering truck that sells hotdogs or mini donuts, you may do well here if there are enough vendors and customers.

- If you sell low priced items, you may do well because flea market goods often do not sell for more than a few dollars.

- There are often fewer requirements or rules, making it easy for you to just show up and sell.

- It is usually less expensive to rent a table at a flea market than at regular markets. Most flea markets are very casual and do not require much in the way of fancy displays.

DISADVANTAGES

- Most customers only come with a few dollars to spend.

- Many customers have a hobby collecting certain items, and have blinders on for anything else on sale.

- If your products are expensive, your items likely will not fit in. Most often, people going to flea markets are looking for inexpensive bargains and collectables.

COMBINATION FARMERS' AND CRAFT MARKETS

Most of the markets I know are of this variety for the simple reason that living in the northern latitudes means that there is limited fresh produce available until late May or June, peaking in July and August. As most markets start in April or early May, crafters are often more visible in the spring markets before the farmers have produce to bring to market.

In all likelihood, you will start selling at a combined farmers' and craft market. It is the most common of all market styles. They are either managed by an independent market society or by a town merchants' association.

If it is run by an independent, non-profit market society, all the market fees go into the society and are usually used on advertising and market support.

They are run by a board of directors and members have voting rights. Many markets require vendors to become members, but you get to vote at meetings, volunteer on committees and generally have your opinions heard at open meetings. The downside is that the bureaucracy can be daunting, petty squabbles are common and grudges can last for years.

Merchants' association run markets are often less bureaucratic since there is no board and no member voting. The association collects the fees and handles all of the marketing and infrastructure. While you can certainly request application forms, merchant-run markets often "invite" vendors whom they think would be a good fit. They also often do not take kindly to vendors photocopying the application form and passing it around to others. They want to be the ones to choose who gets invited and who does not, usually because they also have to think about how vendors will fit in with existing town businesses. They can allow whomever they want to attend, including the possibility of resale or import vendors.

It is in their own best interests to create a market that invites as many customers to come as possible. Town merchant run markets can be exceptionally well managed, vibrant and profitable. Store owners often place their goods outside on sidewalks to take part in the market day.

Both are viable options. Just be sure to read their policies and know what the rules and policies are prior to making your decision to apply.

ADVANTAGES

- You can take advantage of a combined market knowing that customers will be there for both food and other items.

- The market appears fuller with both farm and craft vendors. A sense of abundance creates vibrancy and excitement, encouraging customers to spend money.

- Some markets allow you to share a stall with someone else if you do not have enough products to fill a stall.

- A combined market is helpful when there are tourists who may not be interested in buying food, but might love to take home a hand-made craft.

- Most markets insist that the person who *makes* the product must be the person who is in the stall *selling* the product. This fosters accountability and trust between vendors and customers.

DISADVANTAGES

- Two of the most frequent customer complaints are that there are never enough fresh food vendors and there are always too many crafters.

- Many markets do not allow you to leave if you've sold out before the end of the market. Apparently it looks bad when vendors leave, creating gaps in the visual appeal of the market.

- You may not be accepted if you have a store in town or are only there to promote a business you run elsewhere. For example, if you operate a hair salon out of your home, you'll likely not be allowed to set up an "information" stall just to promote your business. If, though, you cut hair *at* the market, then maybe they'll let you in. You usually are not allowed to hire staff to take your place at the markets. The person who makes the item, must be the one who sells it.

SPECIAL EVENTS

These could be festivals, art fairs, outdoor community events, music festivals, country fairs and Christmas Craft Fairs.

These are annual events held over one or more days. The adjudication and application process can be lengthy and complicated, fees can be steep and often have to be paid months in advance. Most of the shows I attend in November have application dates starting as early as December of the previous year, so it is important to keep close track of dates.

You leave your stall set up overnight and will need tent side walls if you are outside. At night you'll need to protect and secure your goods from the weather, vermin and theft. You may have to pay for your own accommodation if the event is far from home and you may need to apply up to a year in advance.

ADVANTAGES

- They can be superb money making events if you have chosen an event carefully.

- You can reach a target market specific to that event.

- If you do not have time to go to a weekly market, a one-time event could work for your schedule. Your set up is once, and take down is once.

- You can make a lot of money in a short, but intense period of time.

DISADVANTAGES

- Long hours, high costs and stiff competition.

- Attending big shows means you need enough money in advance to make enough stock for the show.

- Judging how much stock to bring can be difficult. If you sell out early, you will have nothing left to sell for the rest of the event. Show organizers frown upon this and may not invite you back if you sell out early.

- Special shows are not usually meant for farm produce although they can be excellent for crafts and value-added food products like baking and preserves.

- Bad weather can kill an event even if it is inside.

- Many events allow import vendors who sell cheap items that can undercut artisan products. Be sure to check if they are allowed in the show and find out whether they will be competition for you.

- If the large event fails for any number of reasons, you could be left with a lot of product. Weekly markets may be better if you only have enough money to make a small number of products at a time.

CONCLUSION

Most new vendors ask around to find out what markets tend to be "good" ones. If you are still not sure, then visit a few markets near you; make careful observations of the vendors, customers, flow and energy of the market. You will quickly get a sense of what markets have good energy and lots of customers buying by the number of overflowing shopping bags they are carrying.

Ask lots of questions, try out a few different markets and after one season doing the markets, you will start to get a feel for which markets best suit your products.

Choosing the Right Product to Sell

$\mathcal{T}$he most important decision you have to make is what to sell. Creating a viable line of products will make or break your market experience and can mean the difference between earning a second or even primary income, or struggling to make your stall fee each week. The answer to this lies in understanding what customers want and then providing the products and services they need and crave. At the same time, it is important to stay flexible so you can change your products as customers' needs and wants change. This happens for many reasons and savvy vendors pay attention to what is happening both in their own communities and the world around them.

Unfortunately, we live in challenging economic times and this means that vendors who chose to sell the results of their casual hobbies may find it more difficult to entice customers. For many vendors, simply making back the money they spent on a hobby by selling off a winter's worth of crafts is not resulting in much interest. For those of you who have a hobby and often get the standard response from friends such as, *"Hey, you could sell those at the market!"* I strongly suggest you read this chapter before you commit to doing markets during tough economic times.

Indeed, while your hobby items may be lovely, in tough times you need to really ramp up your display and sales skills, along with adopting current trends that make enough sense to customers to cause them to part with their hard earned money. There is always a place for beautifully made food and craft items, but it is also more crucial now to understand the needs of today's shoppers.

THE NEEDS OF TODAY'S SHOPPERS

You can always spot a weekly market customer on a mission. They come with their shopping bags, empty egg cartons, money ready and they have a determined, focused air that says they mean business. They buy fresh produce, eggs, baked goods, meats and cheeses. They come for fresh food first and any money left over may be spent on an indulgent treat or gift. These customers do make impulse purchases based on what catches their eyes, so creating attractive displays, and offering a warm, personal welcome is critical. Customers also go to the markets as a form of entertainment and the warm sense of community and vibrancy that the environment offers.

As a vendor, you have to decide where you fit in. Are you a fresh produce vendor or crafter? Do you sell weekly staple grocery items, or small indulgences? Do you sell decorative goods, functional crafts or both? Do you make items that are available more cheaply from large, nearby stores? Knowing what category your products are in will help you decide exactly where you are in your customers' priorities for their weekly shopping and will help you plan your marketing strategy.

The first thing to realize is that public markets can help foster personal connections between vendors and customers that rarely occur in impersonal shopping centers. Markets encourage people to spend time strolling outside, absorbing various sights, sounds and aromas. Customers show each other their purchases, share raspberries and show off the new hat they just bought. They chat over coffee and bring friends to a stall to buy the same products they did. The market can enhance a sense of community through the purchase of goods that are made and sold by local vendors. There is great value in helping foster this environment because it is one of the few public places people can go today where they are greeted by name and a genuine smile. You have the *perfect* opportunity to enhance and help build this environment through your attitude and products.

While it is difficult to compete with large multinational corporations on price, your advantage is your ability to add value where they cannot. Value is more than just a concept of price versus quantity. There are intangible aspects to value that you are perfectly situated to enhance. People who shop at markets already have a gut sense of the value of shopping at the market. If you ask customers what value they get out of shopping at markets, they often say that even though prices might be higher than at big shops, they come away feeling good about their purchases. They feel that the quality is higher and there is a satisfaction in knowing exactly who produced the items they bought.

This is a very powerful concept that many large corporations attempt to capture but fall short because their focus is all about profit and rarely about the heart. Even if they attempt to market their businesses as though they really "care" about their customers, most customers aren't really fooled by the rhetoric. How can they *possibly* act from the heart, from a place of love and caring when the majority of products they "train" people to sell are made in foreign factories by workers who will never see any of the profit the company makes?

Customers also perceive value in the simple esthetic pleasures of holding an exquisitely made, blown glass goblet or feeling the softness of a knitted alpaca shawl. They get value in the satisfaction they receive from eating unsprayed or organically grown produce that supports a healthy diet. They also get emotional value in knowing they are supporting local businesses and are directly responsible for helping the community thrive.

We live in a world with constant access to information about our entire planet. By staying abreast of local and worldwide trends, you can anticipate what may or may not happen in your customers' buying habits and flow with those changes as they occur.

LOCAL TRENDS

In the process of developing your products, whether they are earrings or toma-toes, it is important to explore local purchasing trends in the context of what is happening in the world around you. Staying current with important local issues will give you the advantage of anticipating trends. Gerald Celente of the Trends Research Institute says: *"Current events form future trends."* (*www.trendsresearch.com*) Paying attention to what is happening in the world today will help you adjust your product line to meet the demands of tomorrow's con-sumer. Even if it is just a simple shift in marketing, you show your customers that you are savvy to, and appreciative of, the fact that you care about both local and global issues.

One of the greatest advantages of a small market business is the freedom you have to quickly change your product in keeping with changes happening on a broader scale. While it can literally take years for large corporations to capitalize on major trends, it is almost impossible for them to take advantage of small, regionally specific micro-trends. Read your local papers and pay atten-tion to what is happening in your own backyard.

GLOBAL TRENDS

What global issues are getting a lot of media attention? Aging populations, health concerns, the environment and the economy all spawn trends to solve or prevent the problems associated with each issue. You can address the trend of creating physical accessibility for the elderly by creating jewelery with mag-netic clasps. How about selling low sodium, sugar free food items? The trend of eating unsprayed or organic produce can be addressed by showing a list of all the chemicals sprayed onto conventional produce and then showing customers that you have opted to use ladybugs.

Contrasting and comparing how your product improves on what is already in the marketplace shows customers that you are innovative and creative. By simply addressing a trend through signage or information leaflets, the product becomes more relevant to today's concerns.

An example is a vendor selling storage boxes made of reclaimed wood from a 100-year old demolished factory owned by the town's founding family. The vendor uses wood reclaimed from the old building, has a flyer printed with a vintage photo of the factory and provides a brief historical account. Imagine how much more fulfilling it is to buy a box when there is a deeper story attached to the purchase. The customer is not just purchasing a *box*; they are taking home an important piece of history!

In a world of turmoil and difficulty, helping customers rediscover connections to family and history can offer them a palpable sense of comfort, nostalgia, and love. Ponder how different an experience your customers will have when your approach to selling your products encourages this sense of belonging, feeling and reclamation of history. Compare this sense of experiential and moral depth to buying a box made of new wood harvested from a destroyed rainforest and you quickly see the wonderful opportunities open to you.

Working trends into your marketing and using locally sourced or reclaimed materials all help to create a strong, commercially valid product line.

MARKET OBSERVATIONS

Take some time to walk around a local market paying close attention to the customers, where they go, what they are buying and why they seem to be flocking to particular stalls. Watch as they avoid some stalls, and ask yourself why that happened. You will see patterns emerge that tell you what products are in high demand, at what time of day, and what products are slow to sell. The market's pulse changes throughout the day so go right at the start of the market and notice how the energy changes throughout the day.

Look for gaps in the marketplace that your products could fill. Why sell something that 10 other vendors are already selling? Is the market already saturated with certain products? While market managers and adjudication committees are supposed to create a balanced mix of vendors and products, they do not always manage to do this. It is up to you to take a look around and see what people are selling, and more importantly, what is missing and why.

Take notes while you walk around and compare them to the ideas below, keeping in mind that the whole point of the exercise is to find out whether or not there is or is not a need for the product you are thinking of selling. You may also find opportunities for other products you had not even considered.

- Where are people actually spending their money? What are those stalls selling? What did they sell out of and at what time of day did that happen? Did you arrive at 1:00 pm only to find out all the eggs were sold by 11:00 am? Did they bring enough stock to last the day or are they such a small operation that they only had a few items to sell?

- Observe the stalls where people are not selling much. What is on their tables? Are the vendors engaged with customers, smiling, talking or showing their products or are they scowling, ignoring customers, text messaging, reading, or chatting with their neighbor? Are they clean or dirty? Do they have positive or negative energy? How do you feel near their stall? Does their behavior make you feel welcome or do you just want to move on?

- What is missing in the market? You may find a niche you could fill. Ask the market manager if they are looking for any particular type of vendors, or better yet, ask some of the customers. By far the biggest complaint from customers I've heard is that there is a scarcity of produce available in early spring. Could *you* be the vendor who provides the first spring greens to your market? Are there lots of plants for sale, but no planters? What would you improve if you could?

- Do you see twelve jewelers all making the same kind of thing? The second biggest complaint I hear from customers is that there are too many jewelers. Create something *different* from the others. Versatility, innovation, exceptional quality and value are always appreciated. Customers are more encouraged to buy items that they *cannot* make themselves so try to avoid the cliché "beads-on-a-string" kind of pieces that are available everywhere.

- Does someone's stall resemble a garage sale table packed with a mish mash of unrelated products? Is this stall attracting customers or not? Just because someone might be chatting with a vendor does not actually mean they are buying. Keep your eyes on where the money is going.

- If you have to ask, *"What do you sell?"* then the vendor has not effectively displayed their products. Do they have clear, easy to read signs or do you have to go right up to the table and squint at a tiny sign?

- Notice which vendors have embraced current trends and how they did it. Are they using and promoting recycled materials? Do their signs clearly advertise a particular trend? Look for a repetition of trends throughout the market and imagine how you could use the same or a similar trend. Is there a trend that is obviously missing that you could use and would be of service to your customers?

- Who are the customers at the market? Are they city or country folk? Are they of a specific ethnicity, heritage or religious background, locals or tourists? Are they young, elderly, families or singles? (What is the point of selling 15 lb bags of carrots in a university town full of students who eat at the campus cafeteria?) Try to anticipate their needs and wants, and provide products and pack sizes that suit the *majority* of your customers.

A note here. Customers will *always* ask you to make something you do not have, and often once you actually make it, they will not buy it. Stick to your vision, try out different things, but in the end, create a product line that makes sense to the majority of your customers.

- Are vendors selling only one product or a variety of products? What is the mix of products within each stall? Note the range of prices within a given stall. You may find that a $2,500 sculpture may draw customers into a stall, but customers end up buying the more affordable $40 pieces.

- Which vendors have a wireless point of sale device (POS) that processes both debit and credit card transactions? Ask these vendors if they find the service worthwhile compared to the cost of such a machine. Is there a cash machine or open banks close to the market? Are they food or craft vendors? Customers always run out of cash so if you are a craft vendor, you may want to accept debit and credit cards because people rarely, if ever, come back when they say they have to go to the bank to get more cash.

- What other services are vendors offering? Do they help customers to their cars with their purchases, do they gift wrap, deliver, or customize the products in any way? Ask vendors how often customers take advantage of these services. Sometimes simply *offering* the service is enough to impress customers while they may never even use the service. How many times have you purchased something that came with a coupon or mail-in rebate only to never follow through on redeeming the coupon? It is the *sentiment* that often convinces a customer. Just make sure that you are fully able to follow through on any service you choose to offer!

- Pay attention to what the busy vendors are doing right. Watch their body language, listen to their voices and watch their faces. Do they have warm, welcoming personalities? Do they have a stall that displays their products at their best? Do they have a range of prices that you notice customers responding well to? Can you apply some of their techniques, styles and ways of doing things to your own product line?

You may notice that a particular type of vendor is missing, and you can fill that niche nicely. Or, you may find that the products you were thinking of selling are going to be up against some tough, professional, and *established* competition. There is often considerable customer loyalty to particularly trusted vendors. What *else* can you make that will not be in direct competition with the established vendors, but will still provide value and fill a niche?

In your search through the markets, you will likely find that most of the busy vendors are laughing, talking, smiling and standing up as they attend to customers. Some are quieter, to be sure, but so often the lively, entertaining, but focused, vendors are also those who pay attention to their customers, are efficient with their time, and close sales as soon as they can. They are also focused on *selling*, not chit chatting with their neighbors or huddled in a blanket reading a newspaper. They also often remember people's names and personal details like whether they'd just gotten back from a holiday or if the customers' kids are graduating that year. It is the personal attention that surprises people and some vendors have a real gift for multi-tasking. Pay attention to what they do, how they do it, and try to incorporate some of the techniques they use.

Once you've had a chance to observe a few markets, it is time to look deeper into what drives people to make purchases of your particular products.

RESEARCH, RESEARCH, RESEARCH

Gather more information on what trends and unusual opportunities might work for your particular product:

- Research magazines specific to your product. Magazines are an excellent way of seeing what is current. There are magazines for every conceivable food, craft, art, or farming practice. Check near the backs of these magazines for lists of suppliers, other publications and resources.

- Just because something is not being grown or currently produced in your area, it does not automatically mean that it cannot be. Look into your town archives or interview seniors to find out what *used* to be grown or made where you live. You could be part of the growing trend to reclaim diversity through heritage crops, livestock or traditional arts and crafts once well known in your area.

- Women still do most of a family's shopping, so cater to their needs for convenience, versatility and value. The last thing you want to offer is a product that will end up creating even more work for a busy mother.

- Men's interests and needs are often neglected at the markets. Are there any products that will appeal to the men in your area? Is your community known for any particular sport, recreational activity or industry for which you can provide products? For example, in a fly-fishing community can you make hand tied flies attached to a photo card of a local fish that likes to eat this fly? Can you provide both products and education for the fly-fishing tourist and local alike? This section does not have to apply to men's interests only.

- Scan local and national television shows for trends and frequently repeated buzz words. Find some way that these trends fit your products, or create a product that fits the trends knowing full well that this trend might last for only one season. Avoid investing huge amounts of money developing products with no staying power, especially with regard to fashion items like accessories.

- Surf the Internet for trends in flavors, scents, colors, fashions, farming, gardening, and anything else that might influence how your products are viewed by the public. Type in simple searches like farming trends, flavor trends, craft trends. Check out product specific blogs. Bloggers are often quicker to spot trends than magazines since magazines have to create their issues months in advance of the actual publication dates.

CHOOSING PRODUCTS CUSTOMERS WANT TO BUY

Try to create products that appeal to a wide range of customers. This is hard to do if you only sell baby bibs, but you could make matching aprons for mom or dad, and in this way you expand your market to include adults.

- Are you a massage therapist, reiki practitioner, tarot card reader, reflexologist? Many markets will have at least a few service-oriented vendors, some of whom might offer special deals to other vendors.

- Multi-use or transformable items are gaining popularity as well. Pants with legs that zip off to create shorts, bags that turn into rain ponchos, jewelry with interchangeable parts and garden furniture that doubles as storage are all examples of products that do more than one thing. Provide instructions!

- Play up the idea of a **small indulgence**. People will pay a premium for a small chocolate truffle to give themselves a treat, but may feel guilty if they bought a whole box for themselves. They might not want to spend a lot of money on a huge bouquet of flowers, but will happily go home with a delicate posy nestled in a vintage teacup. Many people, especially women, do not feel entitled to treat themselves to something special when they are use to putting their family's needs first. Offering a small indulgence, even if the cost is higher per unit, is sometimes all a customer needs to feel like they treated themselves to something special. You are providing a sense of indulgence with a minimum of guilt.

- The power of *cute* and *small* cannot be underestimated. While a 100 pound pumpkin is impressive and draws a crowd, good luck selling the darn thing. In a world over saturated with mega-sized everything, it is refreshing to find products that are small again. Gigantic does not always mean good quality or value if it only ends up going to waste and creating a sense of guilt. People love baby potatoes, early greens, fresh, young beans and corn, and of course, the first tender strawberry.

- When people squeal at your stall and clutch an adorable little stuffed bunny made of recycled eco-friendly materials, you've captured the "cuteness factor" as well as the current trend of reusing materials. There is a sense of childhood innocence in the appreciation of small, cute things that conjures up days of freedom and safety. In an increasingly chaotic world, people appreciate a gentle smile all wrapped up in a perfect little package.

Two cute ceramic geese

- Consumable items that a customer uses and replenishes create repeat customers. Selling starter packs of sample sizes of products like soaps, creams and cleaning supplies gives customers a chance to test your products before committing to larger volumes. Package them in boxes, cello bags or reusable packaging tied with beautiful ribbon to make easy gifts. If you want to use recycled packaging, then spray painting the boxes all the same color or using matching ribbon will help create a cohesive look.

Products packaged in cello bags make gift
giving easier for the customer

- Use the power of a focus group to help you decide which product may sell best for you. Make several versions of your product; invite 8-10 people who you would define as your ideal customer and ask them to rate your products based on specific criteria you create. Family members or close friends may not give honest reactions so you might have to get someone else to conduct the session for you. Have the criteria anonymously compiled so no one in the group will feel like they are attacking you. This can be an excellent way of assessing your products before you release them to the public. I've done this with every product I've created and it is usually a lot of fun too.

- If your market consists primarily of locals, selling "one-off" items may quickly saturate the marketplace. A one-off item is something like a garden bench or birdbath. Once they buy one, how many more do customers actually need? Diversify your product line by including coordinating accessories or refills. Do you make handbags out of recycled leather jackets? Great, then add coordinating cell phone cases, eye glass cases, zippered cosmetics pouches and agenda covers. Do you make garden furniture? Why not also make cushions made with weatherproof fabric?

- It is sometimes hard to make a living with only one product so develop variations on a theme. If you sell aprons, then make one pattern from a variety of materials. If you sell eggplant, then sell as many varieties as you can grow. Sell them individually or in a mixed bag so people can try them all.

- At the beginning of each market season, customers always want to know what you have that is new. It is more prudent to introduce one or two items at a time with great fanfare than flood the market with ten new products all at once. Plan on adding at least one new product a season and drop any products that do not sell as well as you'd hoped.

- If you are going to make something that is more cheaply available in large retail stores, then make yours different. Can it be made of recycled materials? Can you improve it in some way? Is there really a need for more of these items around or is the general marketplace covered? If you notice that no one is selling a particular item, find out *why* before you invest your time and money in a product that possibly no one wants or needs. A good example of this is the influx of vendors selling reusable fabric shopping bags. You can buy them at grocery stores for under a dollar and yet, the ones available at market are often not much different. Never have I seen a reusable shopping bag with a waterproof, washable liner, or with bottle pockets. I have never seen a bag with cooler linings to keep eggs and cheeses cool. If you do not make your products better than what is out there, why would anyone buy it?

While many of the above suggestions can be adapted to craft and food vendors alike, there are some specific suggestions for each category that are good to know.

CRAFTS AND ARTISTIC PRODUCTS

If you want an honest opinion on your work, avoid asking your family. They are likely not trained artisans, do not want to hurt your feelings and it is really not fair to do this to them if you are sensitive and emotionally attached to your work. In fact, ask yourself *why* you are attached to your work. With experience, you will find that it often becomes easier to let go of items and focus on the joy that they will give to others as opposed to focusing on losing part of your soul by giving something up. Ask an art teacher or a gallery owner who is not already a good friend of yours to make honest suggestions that would help improve the quality and execution of your craft. Be prepared to take a close look at your own work. Be committed to growth and constantly seek to refine your skills.

Be wary of those who would criticize your work too harshly without offering concrete suggestions for improvement. There are those people out there who find talented artisans a threat to their own creativity. Follow your gut and listen when it tries to tell you that someone is jealous or may be putting up barriers to your own success. You may find that the artists you've asked for help may be struggling themselves and are jaded by the years of struggle. Do not let these negative people deter you.

I was told by a previously published author that no one ever makes money self-publishing a book. She honestly felt that she needed to warn me about putting too much hope into making my money back on this book because she never did. If I had allowed that one person to dissuade me, the book you are holding in your hands right now would not exist. Another thing she failed to realize is that my reasons for writing this book aren't really about making money at all. It's about service. Sure, it'd be nice to make back the money I spent on this book, but that's not my main objective.

Remember, too, that your product is only part of the equation of success. Your display, price points, attitude and sales techniques account for a lot of your success. If you are blessed with exceptional sales skills and personal warmth, you may be able to compensate for mediocre product and lackluster stall design. However, most people need to create a balanced approach of continually developing craft skills, honing sales techniques, and adjusting their stall design to best display their products.

VALUE-ADDED FOOD PRODUCTS

Creating value-added food products is the process of taking a food ingredient and adding *value* to it by processing it into something else. Strawberries turned into jam is a good example. Value-added food products can mean the difference between a limited seasonal income selling fresh produce and one that provides a year round income. Many farm vendors make preserves throughout the year and supplement fresh food sales with pickles, chutneys, jams and sauces. If there is a glut of certain kinds of produce, they make preserves instead of throwing the remaining product to the pigs or into the compost. They also often sell at Christmas fairs near the end of the year when customers are looking for Christmas gifts. Some vendors even manage to find shops that will sell their preserves on consignment or will buy them at wholesale. Doing this expands the vendor's season into the winter months when selling out of doors becomes impractical due to cold weather.

Beautifully presented preserves

Make products that customers cannot find among the generic varieties at large supermarkets. Why make Dijon style mustard if you can buy it much cheaper in town? Make more exotic mustard instead. If you make strawberry jam then make a batch with liquors or spices like cardamom, chili peppers or flavorings that may be part of a current flavor trend.

Create something that is a touch different, but not intimidating to customers if you live in a conservative area. Do not sacrifice flavor and marketability for excessive cleverness. Make a small batch of a product and have your customers try it. You'll discover very quickly if they like it, and then you can decide whether or not to make more.

One other piece of advice I've received is to make products from ingredients you can always buy at the grocery store. If the grocery store can get the ingredients all the time, then you should be able to get them at wholesale prices from distributors. If you choose ingredients that come from far away, shipping costs are often quite high. Keep about a three-month supply of ingredients and packaging on hand. Find out if there are times of the year when the ingredients are more difficult to get so you can plan your purchases.

You may need to invest in a large freezer to store excess produce purchased in season. It's often very difficult for busy vendors to sell at markets *and* do production when produce is in season. There is a limited time window in which one can harvest and process so many vendors freeze ingredients until they're ready to process. Make sure ingredients are clearly marked as to where they came from and when they were harvested and frozen.

PEOPLE LOVE A GOOD STORY

For customers, going to a market is an experience and holds an incomparable nostalgia. Visitors, tourists and even locals love it when you have interesting (but *short*) stories attached to your products. Tell the story of how your grandmother made and sold jam to help your family survive during the 1930's. Your customers will feel a sense of history and connection to you, especially if they have similar stories. Put a photo of your grandmother making the jam onto your label. If you have a sample of her handwriting, copy and use it across the corner of your brochure. It will give the impression of family history that many people treasure. With scrap booking resources available everywhere, you can create prototypes that can then be scanned and printed onto labels, brochures, signs and banners.

Create products that say something about who you are. This can foster camaraderie between you and your customers, through family, through history, through culture, and you'll be creating an experience for customers that is above and beyond anything they expected. It will be *memorable*, and that, more than anything else, is what is missing from mainstream stores. When was the last time you came home from a large commercial store with a warm sense of community and historical connection?

CONCLUSION

Many vendors decide to sell products at the market because they are simply trying to sell off items that they've made as a hobby. People tell them, *"Hey, you could sell those!"* They knitted twenty scarves during the winter so they decide it'd be a good idea to sell them. They grew way too many zucchinis so they think of unloading them at the market.

This, in and of itself, is just as valid a reason for going to the market as someone who spent a considerable amount of time researching and planning a product line. What often happens, though, is that someone's personal hobby may not be of much interest to customers. The products may be difficult to sell if there is no connection with current trends, they are out of season, or are carelessly marketed. Simply plunking down a few items on a bare table and expecting them to sell is becoming increasingly difficult in tough economic times. Quite frankly, it also makes the market look bad and generally lowers the overall quality and appeal of the market. When a market starts looking like a flea market, the higher end customers looking for excellence in craft and food tend to go elsewhere.

Customers need enticement to part with their shrinking discretionary money and that means that it's in everyone's best interests to pull up your socks and create the best quality products you can show in a beautiful display. Researching current trends and local and global issues will help you adopt some popular issues into your marketing and make your products more relevant in today's marketplace.

Familiarize yourself with the market environment by going as a customer. Pay attention to what is selling, how the vendors behave and what is missing at the market that might offer you opportunities for your own market business. Create connections for customers based on history, community and show them how your products address some of the more important issues we face today. A final question to ask yourself is this: *"Would I buy this if I were walking around a market and saw it on a table?"*

Can you be the first to market with early strawberries?

Setting Up Your Business

*T*here are several ways of setting up your business. The easiest is to simply make some products, rent a table and start selling. It does not usually require any special forms, bank accounts or registration and may be an option if you just want to see if market life appeals to you. You can always set up a more formal business arrangement later as your sales grow. There are, however, some basic financial considerations to make if you want to keep on the good side of the tax authorities.

MANAGING YOUR FINANCES

Basically, it is important to keep track of your business expenses and revenues, and collect any relevant sales taxes to submit to the government at the appropriate time of the year. You may or may not be subject to charging and submitting sales taxes so check with your tax authority to be certain of the laws where you live.

While most banks would prefer you to open a proper business account if you have a market business, check whether there are any laws that actually require you to do this. You might simply be able to use a regular checking account, keep all your receipts for business expenses, deposit market revenue and then pay the business bills from that account. You can deposit money into a dedicated account as initial capital and start your accounting books from there. As long as you keep accurate records of money coming in and out of your business, collect and submit the appropriate taxes, you should be fine come tax time.

There are some basic things to keep in mind when you are running a market business:

- While it is pretty easy to set up a business, it is often more challenging to rein in your initial spending, especially when you are flush with set up money. It's really tempting to spend money on relatively useless things. Avoid buying equipment like a brand new truck and having it painted with your company name if you are only selling at the market. If you need a truck now and again, then why not rent one on a weekly basis instead of buying one? It will likely be cheaper than buying it! It is easy to get sucked into buying expensive equipment and supplies you really do not need. Buy the minimum of what you need, and look into borrowing, renting or leasing equipment until you are certain of what you really need.

- If a dealer or supplier comes to you with a great deal, always ask for references and *call* them. Sales people always make it sound like it is now or never and you'll be losing out on a life changing deal if you do not buy from them. Do not fall for it. There will *always* be another deal down the road when you are ready and have enough experience to know what equipment will really work to increase productivity and reduce costs. That is the only reason to buy equipment in the first place! If it takes you twenty years to amortize the cost of a piece of equipment when you are uncertain about the financial viability of your small market business, then do not buy it.

- Always, ALWAYS, get more than one quote for any kind of business service you are looking at, be it labels, packaging, financial services, supplies or equipment. Ask if set up fees can be waived, and if it is the best deal you can get. There are often deals and specials to be had on equipment, supplies, etc, but it is better to buy less of something initially than pay for a huge supply of something that you may never use.

- Deposit *all* market revenue into your dedicated bank account. Then transfer money into a personal account before you use it so you can keep track of your total revenues compared to your personal income. If you bring in $20 cash at the market, do not take it out of your cash box and then go buy that night's dinner. If you need to "borrow" money out of your cash box, write yourself an IOU and then repay the cash box later from personal funds. If you take cash out of your business account, make sure you use it only for business and keep all receipts. Some of you may scoff at this because you may feel that no one will know if you do not declare that income. Do your research. Know the tax laws where you live and be prepared to answer tough questions should you be questioned by the tax authority on your business practices.

- Do not use your business account for personal expenses and then claim it was a business expense. An example of that would be going out to a movie with your family, paying for it using your business debit card, and then entering that into your books under "entertainment expenses." All you really need to do is ask yourself a simple question every time you use your business account. *"Would I be able to justify this as a business purchase to the tax authority?"* If you cannot, then use a different account. If you are not sure whether a purchase would be considered business or personal, ask a competent business accountant or call your local tax office to help you.

- If you have to charge sales taxes on your products, make sure to separate the tax monies owed to the government from your revenues and then submit the taxes when you have to. Find out whether you can include the tax in your price or whether there are any laws requiring that taxes always be added separately onto a bill. If you do include taxes in your retail price, make sure that you clearly post this on your pricing sheet.

- Stay on top of your bookkeeping. One simple way is to use large manila envelopes with the month and year written on them and put all of your paid business bills and receipts into the envelopes. Put receipts and paid bills into the envelope as you get them so they do not get lost in a heap of mail or papers on your desk. At the end of each month, either enter the amounts yourself into a set of books or bookkeeping software, or give the receipts to your bookkeeper or accountant. Some do the books monthly, while others do it quarterly or even yearly. A good idea to save time and money is to organize and tally your receipts according to the categories you set up for business. That way, the bookkeeper does not have to keep asking you what each individual receipt is for.

- Invest in a good shredder. Shred all papers prior to putting into recycling to avoid identity theft. It is important to safeguard your personal life and business. Just be sure to know how long you have to hold onto business and legal records prior to disposal!

Consider buying a safe and having it installed properly into your home office. Keep all valuable legal documents as well as customer credit card slips, market revenues or float money in there in case of break-ins.

As your business grows, registering your business can provide some benefits. Creating a legal business can give you access to supplies at wholesale prices, rental of point of sale devices and discounts on various business fees. There might also be some tax benefits, access to business loans, funding grants and other capital investment that might not be available to you if you do not have a registered business.

Remember though, the more you involve government or corporate agencies to "help" in your business, the more paperwork they are likely to require. Make sure you spend considerable time assessing your needs as compared to whether the money and support gained is worth the extra time and effort you'll need to administrate the entire affair.

CREATING A LEGAL BUSINESS

You may still have to apply for a business license or some other permits, but basically, all you need to get going is the desire to do it. At the end of the year, file your personal income tax and declare any business revenues if required. Your tax accountant, bookkeeper or tax authority will be able to advise you on what you are legally required to do so be sure to consult with someone competent for the proper legal advice.

Once you get to the stage where you want a more formal business structure, there are some relatively simple tasks to get you going. There are many good detailed resources available through local government agencies so there is really no need to go into them here in detail. Visit your municipal office or even your local library. Ask them where you can find information for setting up a small business. They should be able to point you in the right direction.

Here is a basic list of what is commonly needed to set up a legal business structure.

1. Get a name search done for your business if you are using any name other than your own.

2. Check with the local tax authority, a business lawyer or your book-keeper or accountant to find out what tax numbers you'll be required to apply for.

3. Choose your business structure and register it.

4. Apply for any business licenses, permits and health forms you'll need.

5. Get liability insurance including general commercial liability and product insurance if you need it.

6. Create a set of accounting books.

7. Open a business bank account.

BUSINESS NAME

A business name search is easy. Pick three possible business names. Complete a name search form and find out if you are legally allowed to use any of those names. Someone else may have already chosen the first name you want so you will not be able to use it. Sometimes you can apply for a name search online, or get a paper application that you fill out and send in.

Read the details and name creation suggestions on the form and make sure you pick at least three possibilities you can live with. Make sure your name conveys what you make, but avoid limiting yourself by stating that you make only one product. If you bake and sell cupcakes, and your chosen name is "The Cupcake Kid" that is adorable, but limiting. What happens if you decide to start making cookies or pies as well? At the same time, a name like, "ABC Foods" is not very exciting and says nothing about what you sell.

TAXES

Depending on where you live and what you are selling, you may be required to collect and submit taxes on each sale. You may also be able to recover some sales taxes that you have to pay when purchasing items for your business, including taxes paid on packaging materials, services etc. If you're not a registered business, you will likely not able to claim back any of these expenses. There is usually a minimum amount of revenue your business must make in order to qualify to receive back some of the taxes you pay on goods or services related to your business. Canada Revenue Agency (CRA) and the Internal Revenue Service (IRS) both have extensive websites. An accountant or business lawyer should be able to help you as well. Do this before you register because you need to know what tax numbers to apply for before you register your business.

TYPES OF BUSINESSES

There are various legal entities under which your business can operate, each with its own set of advantages and disadvantages. A business lawyer or accountant can explain the pros and cons, and there are many good references online and available through your government access centers to guide you. In a nutshell, here are three basic options.

SOLE PROPRIETORSHIPS

As a sole proprietor, *you* are considered the business and are personally responsible for any liabilities attributed to the business. You set your own goals, keep all the after tax profits and you alone get to enjoy the fruits of your labor after the government takes its cut. The important thing is to learn to recognize when to do certain types of work yourself and when to hire professional help. One of the biggest mistakes people make is to try to do absolutely everything themselves. This can lead to lost time, mistakes and serious burn out. A wise sole proprietor knows that it will often save time and money in the long run if competent people are paid to do some of your work for you.

While most vendors have to be the ones to make and then sell their own wares, that doesn't mean you can't pay people to do some other tasks. I have used the services of an accountant, chemist, business consultant, web designers, photographers and graphic designers. All of the work these professionals do would have been impossible for me to do unless I invested in years of study. Do yourself a favor. Recognize the tasks you either cannot or don't like to do, and pay someone to do them for you. File your personal tax return and include business revenues and a statement of business activities on the advice of a competent small business accountant. You may or may not have to pay income tax depending on your overall income. You may also be able to file later in the year than if you did not have a registered business. Check with your tax authority on what laws are applicable to where you live and the type of business structure you have.

PARTNERSHIPS

The benefits of a partnership are in combined capital, shared labor, collaborative ideas and varied skills. There can be a wonderful synergy between partners that simply cannot occur when you fly solo. It can be exciting and a lot of fun, but partnerships can also be fraught with problems and legal hassles if the details are not carefully thought through.

A general partnership is like a sole proprietorship, but with two or more owners. Owners file their personal tax returns just like a sole proprietor. The key to a successful partnership is in the clarity and depth of the written agreement between the partners.

This is one area in which I would recommend a skilled business lawyer to help you draft up a clear and complete agreement so that all of the partners are clear about expectations, responsibilities and risks. While it certainly is an option to write up your own agreement and have it properly notarized, be sure you've done considerable research before signing. Personally, if a potential partner were unwilling to work on an official agreement, I would hesitate to get involved.

LIMITED LIABILITY COMPANY

The premise for creating a limited company is that the business is a separate legal entity from you. This means that your personal assets are protected from any creditor with a claim against the business. There can also be some tax benefits, but overall, the hassle and expense is usually not worth the effort for a small market business. In some cases a limited company is still not ironclad protection in case of litigation. Most small market businesses do just fine with a simpler legal structure. Again, do your homework, check with competent and experienced business lawyers and accounts and decide what would work best for your situation.

BUSINESS LICENSES, PERMITS AND INSURANCE

Municipalities have business by-laws and zoning requirements so check with your city or regional office to see what permits or licenses you need if you want to run your business from home or at another location.

If you are operating a food production business from your home, there are usually guidelines available from your local public health office to help you make your products at a minimum standard of food safety. Some markets still allow vendors to sell items made at home, but often require informing customers that products are not made in a commercially inspected kitchen. Make sure to educate yourself on the difference between a guideline and a law as health inspectors from different jurisdictions often interpret "guidelines" differently. Approval in one area may be different in another depending on who is administering the guidelines or laws. If at all possible, get any stipulations or requirements in writing so that you know exactly what you need to do so you can refer back to the requirements in case random or arbitrary changes are made. It happens all the time. Someone says you need to do something while you talk to them on the phone and then you find out later that the whole scenario has changed depending on who you talk to. Get it in writing!

General commercial liability insurance is something to consider buying. Most markets carry their own insurance to cover you if someone trips and falls in your stall, but not if someone claims they got sick or were injured by your products. That is a separate designation called "product insurance" so check with your insurance broker on whether that is covered under your general liability policy, and whether or not you feel the cost of insurance is justified by the kind of products you sell. Never just take an insurance broker's word that product insurance is included. Make sure they show you the relevant passages within the insurance documents that prove it.

BOOKKEEPING

Keeping accurate financial records is important and many vendors do their own bookkeeping. There is good software available or you can use a simple spreadsheet. Others just do it manually with a set of books bought at an office supply store.

Always keep hard copy printouts of your monthly books, or backup your files on removable flash drives so that if anything should ever happen to your main computer, you will not have lost your data. Keep any backup data in a different secure location from your main computer in case of fire or other disasters. This is prudent for all your personal information and part of any reasonable emergency preparedness plan.

Paying a bookkeeper to help you set up a simple system will keep you organized and is well worth the money if you are not sure how to do it. It sure beats sorting through a big pile of receipts at the end of the year!

BUSINESS BANK ACCOUNT

You do not necessarily need to open a business bank account, but some banks will provide you a business line of credit or business credit cards at reasonable rates that can help you with cash flow. Business banking fees can be quite high so make sure you look through the fees carefully before you decide. You can order business checks through the bank but it is usually cheaper to order through office supply stores.

CONCLUSION

Save yourself any potential legal hassles by doing it right the first time. Being a vendor is a lot of fun, but it can be a real headache if you mix business and personal finances.

Beyond the legal ramifications of not declaring market revenue, if you use gross market revenue to pay for personal expenses, it will be difficult to ever get an accurate picture of your business revenue and expenses. If you ever plan on selling the business in the future, how will you truly value your business if you don't have accurate financial records?

Just as you file your tax return every year, you are also responsible for creating and keeping accurate records. You should be able to prove what monies came into and out of your business regardless of whether or not it is a registered company. Many people avoid this initial step because they do not really know what to do.

Most important:

Do your homework and only take calculated risks.

Never let anyone push you into making a decision until you can clearly identify the benefits and risks.

Go slowly – take your time when deciding what to do for *your* business.

Managing Production Space

$\mathcal{O}$nce you've decided what to sell, you need to find a place where you can make your products. It is a good idea, in fact, to consider your production space needs at the same time as you are planning your product line. You could have a fantastic idea for a product only to discover that you cannot find anywhere to make it.

This chapter will cover both food and craft vendors with specific sections for both. I recommend reading through the entire chapter because some concepts apply to both.

FRESH FOOD PRODUCERS

It helps if you have a farm or even a big backyard where you are able to grow, harvest, sort, rinse off your produce, pack up your truck and head to market. Keep all chemicals away from where you are sorting, packing or storing produce. Keep produce off the floor and pests under control.

If you process the products in some way, like washing and bagging lettuce greens, you may be subject to health regulations. Meats, fish, dairy products and eggs are usually subject to a variety of regulations so check with your local public health authority to help guide you to the correct laws regulating your particular products.

VALUE-ADDED FOOD PRODUCTION

Most people who start small food businesses initially do it out of their home kitchens. As you grow, however, you may eventually want to find a commercial kitchen in which to make your product. A commercial kitchen is an officially inspected kitchen where someone makes products that are usually meant for someone else as an end user. Restaurants, hospital kitchens and school kitchens are all examples of commercial kitchens. They are inspected and approved by various health inspection agents and approval permits should be posted in visible areas. Some products will need basic lab tests for pH and bacterial counts to prove that they are safe to consume. Many public health boards provide guidelines to help vendors produce safely.

Value-added food products are ranked as low to high risk. They include spice or baking mixes, jams, preserves, packaged goods, dry goods, and baking. Some products are stable and safe at room temperature, like dry spice mixes, other products, risk developing bacteria if left out of a refrigerator for more than an hour or two, while most canned products need to be adequately processed or they could develop pathogenic contamination. You need to make and sell healthy products, but with a minimum of care it is not all that difficult.

Develop standard, simple, common sense protocols to control the most obvious health and safety issues. More detailed codes of practice can be found by contacting state, provincial or federal health boards.

SAFE FOOD PROTOCOLS

The following minimum requirements should be followed whether you do production in your home or at a rented commercial kitchen:

- Keep animals out of the kitchen as you work.

- Ingredients should be stored at the temperature stated on their packaging. They should be kept off the floor, and in storage away from pets, dirt, bugs, rodents and litter boxes.

- You should also record every ingredient's lot # and expiry or best before dates and enter those numbers onto a batch production sheet for each batch of product you make. Then assign a lot # and expiry or best before date for each product you make and put these numbers onto each and every label. This will ensure that you can track every single product you make in case something goes wrong with a particular batch. Not including lot numbers means that if something goes wrong, you have to issue a total recall of every single product you make.

- Wear a chef's uniform or long white lab coats to cover your clothes. Wash and store them separately from other clothing.

- Wear non-skid, closed-toe supportive shoes.

- Wear hairnets (and beard nets if you have facial hair) and use non-latex, un-powdered gloves. Get them at janitor or hospital supply stores. Nitril is a common material used in non-latex gloves.

- Disinfect all surfaces using sterilized cleaning cloths and health board approved cleaners with accelerated hydrogen peroxide (Oxygenic) or a bleach and water solution. Make sure you have adequate ventilation when using these products.

- Do not eat, drink or smoke in the production area. Keep all drinks and snacks away from the production area.

- Do not wear any jewelry and take off any nail polish that may chip and fall into food. Some people cannot get their rings off, so use gloves if this is the case. Keep hands scrupulously clean and scrub under your fingernails. Wash your hands with hot soapy water each time you sneeze, rub your nose, or go to the bathroom. If you have to sneeze or cough, turn your head away from whatever you are cooking and sneeze or cough into your sleeve. If you are cooking products that are particularly spicy, wear a dust mask and goggles to prevent eye and nose irritation.

- Use clean spoons for sampling and never lick your fingers to sample product or wipe jar rims or lids. Always use clean utensils when measuring out ingredients.

If you are not sure if a procedure is food safe or not, consult with your local health inspector. You can always also ask yourself this simple question: *"If a health inspector were standing behind me right now, would he or she approve of what I am doing?"* You can also ask a food chemist or you may find a food processing association nearby where they may offer some auditing services where they come to your production facility and help you fine tune your production systems.

FINDING PRODUCTION SPACE

When you are doing production, try to focus on that task alone. Time your production activities so you know just how much labor to add to your costing. If you are busy doing lots of other things around the house at the same time, it is difficult to know the true cost of making your products.

PRODUCING IN YOUR OWN HOME

Many fledgling vendors simply do production out of a spare room, basement, garage, shed or kitchen. This is an excellent way to get started because it does not cost you anything. You can usually work at whatever time of day you'd like barring any particularly noisy activities that may disturb family or neighbors.

Here are some important considerations:

- Check with a business accountant on whether you can deduct part of your rent, mortgage or utilities for using part of your house for business.

- If you live in a condo or apartment, there may be rules about running a business from your unit. You may need board approval before you start.

- Be aware of any noise or pollution your business makes. Most municipalities have by-laws to protect citizens from noise or pollutants.

- You may also need a business license if you run your business from your home.

- If you live with others, keep your business materials in one spot and try not to take over the whole house.

- Set rules about working time and family time, and create a family plan so that everyone understands when you need to focus on your work. It is always challenging to work from home, especially if you are doing it between trips back and forth to soccer, making dinner and laundry.

Many families start a market business to generate income while staying home with young children. It can work really well if you are organized and have clear goals. If, however, you are finding that your business is taking over the house, garage, shed and every other nook and cranny in the house, it may be time to start looking for a place to rent.

RENTING COMMERCIAL SPACE

There are many places for rent on an as-needed basis. Basically, you rent it when you need to do a whole bunch of production at one time. That's what I've been doing for the past ten years and it's worked well for me. Some people only need to rent a facility once in a while, so it is a good alternative to working from home.

Owners of commercial spaces are usually worried about equipment being broken, renters leaving a mess, theft or failure to pay. This is because people rarely, if ever, treat other people's property with respect. You will have to show them that you are responsible. If you follow my suggestions below, you will have a better chance at securing a space than if you simply called up and asked if you could rent their space.

When you approach the owners of a commercial space, think of it like a job interview and come prepared with the following:

- A list of products you are going to make and what equipment you need.

- A list of references that speak to your cleanliness and trustworthiness.

- A written agreement that states that you will pay for repairs or replacement of any equipment you damage.

- After an initial trial period, if you and the owners are satisfied with how you are using the space, have them sign a formal agreement to continue renting the space to you. If they change their minds, you should be given several months' notice to allow you to find another production facility. You are at the mercy of the owners of these facilities, but with signed and witnessed agreements you may have some legal recourse should things go sour.

- Ask them to train you on equipment you are going to use and get a contact list for repairs in case of emergencies or breakdown of equipment.

- Be willing to accept that your rental times may vary and may even be late at night or on weekends. Plan to make as much product as you can at one time.

- If your products take longer to finish than the day you've rented, ask if you can rent or bring in lockable storage. Find out if their insurance covers your property or if you'll need your own.

LOOKING FOR RENTAL SPACE

- Ask other vendors where they do production and if they will give you contact information. Some vendors own their own facilities so may be willing to rent it out to you. You might borrow or rent space from a neighbor or friend.

- Look for Community Kitchens in the yellow pages. These facilities are used to teach people how to cook, preserve foods, make soups and large batch recipes to take home and freeze for later use. They may welcome extra rental revenue.

- Community centers, schools, churches, galleries and production facilities may let you rent space.

- Co-packers are industrial food production facilities offering production services for larger volumes than vendors can make in their homes. If you are allowed to work on the production line with them, you should be able to have the product made there and still be allowed to sell at the market. Remember that most markets have rules that clearly state that the vendor must be the person who makes the product. Co-packing facilities often have minimum run sizes so you will need capital to invest in enough supplies and packaging to make it worth your while. This option is generally only for vendors who intend to wholesale their products as well as do markets because of the volumes required.

- You may try to organize a group rental. If there are a number of artisans in your community, perhaps you can rent a space together. You could rent it yourself and then sublet so that others can use the space. This can work very well as a collaborative artistic environment. However, like general partnerships, there needs to be clear rules and agreements in place to ensure fairness. The last thing you want is to rent a place too expensive for your budget only to have someone back out or fail to pay their rent. Choose your partners wisely.

BUILDING YOUR OWN FACILITY

Some people prefer to build their own production facility. There are government grants available for a lot of different enterprises and it's worth taking a look at what money is available to you. It is a lot of work to build your own space and often full of contradictory regulations. I tend not to recommend this course of action at the beginning stages of a small market business. Wait until you know for certain that your product line is viable and you see consistent sales that match your goals before you venture into construction. Still, it *can* be worth it if your business grows and there are few places around in which to do production.

The advantages of this set up are obvious. You will never have to rely on anyone else for production space and you can buy or lease only the equipment that you need. It is the "dream" scenario for many. If you do choose this route, be sure to get any health or building requirements in writing so you are absolutely certain about what you have to do to satisfy the various regulatory agencies. That may be easier said than done but be forewarned that building your own facility can be a regulatory nightmare. I like to keep it simple and rent someone else's space.

INDUSTRIAL PARKS

If you rent industrial space to do production a number of issues may arise. You will likely have to commit to a lease for anywhere from one to five years.

If you produce items that are sensitive or have special sanitation requirements, be sure to ask pertinent questions if you are considering renting industrial space. If, for example, you bake delicate pastries in a building with shared ventilation, what will you do if someone moves in who uses highly volatile or dangerous chemicals? The smells will permeate your food items and could cause contamination. Ask the following questions:

- What kinds of businesses are allowed to rent here?

- Is the ventilation shared or separate for each unit?

- Is the water supply potable and is there adequate routing to avoid backups into your space?

- Is there access for large delivery trucks, a forklift or pallet jack available, adequate lighting and buzzers for each unit?

- Is there safe parking, adequate surveillance and a security system?

- Can you get a written, legally binding guarantee that no neighbors will be allowed to move in that might compromise your products' safety and quality?

CONCLUSION

This book is about getting your business off the ground as efficiently and economically as possible. If you can start at home, do that and then reassess your space needs as you grow.

Starting your market business can be as simple as clearing space in a spare room and setting up a worktable, or as complicated and expensive as building a production space from scratch.

My suggestion is to start small, using the least amount of space you need. Once you have some experience in making your products, you will realize where you may need more space. If you are fine where you are, why go to the extra expense of renting or leasing outside space? By all means, look for space that may be available, but only rent it if you really need it. Remember that the bigger you get, the more expenses and headache you're likely to have. Growing into a larger business doesn't automatically mean that you will have a more success-ful business. Yes, your revenues may increase, but so will your workload, stress and the chance of complication, especially if you have to hire staff.

While never ending, continual growth and expansion seems to be the dog-matic mantra of the corporate Western society, I find it interesting that it is the only system on the planet that works this way. Everything in life is about birth, growth, maturity and decline. This is more of a philosophical question but it is directly relevant to how people approach the concept of business. Do you want to live a balanced life, where you can make your own products, sell at local markets and have time to relax and enjoy your life? Or do you want to force and push and struggle to grow grow grow only to end up totally exhausted and asking yourself why you started this whole thing in the first place? Think carefully, go slowly, and constantly assess whether you're happy where you are in your market business. Only you can decide.

Costing and Pricing

$\mathscr{F}$or many market vendors, selling at the market is more about supporting a hobby than it is about developing a profitable business. If making a profit is not a priority for you, then feel free to skip this chapter. There may come a day though, when you discover that with just a *little* effort, you can turn your hobby into a viable way of making extra money. I would be remiss, however, in denying the fact that few market vendors make a living solely on market revenue. This is especially true if they have family to care for and doubly so for small farming operations. Most vendors have other jobs or a spouse who pays the bills.

For a rare few, myself included, market and some wholesale revenue is our *only* source of income. This makes sourcing supplies, costing and pricing vitally important if we want to live off this income. For myself, it is sell or fail and that, in itself, is a great motivator to do the very best I can to maximize profits and focus on sales. If you have steady employment with extended medical and dental benefits, paid sick leave or holidays, think very carefully before you let those benefits go to pursue a market business fulltime. Wait until you've seen a track record of steady sales and profits before you take the leap to a fulltime market business.

Most vendors admit that they'd like to make more of a profit, but do not really know the mechanics of costing and pricing. However, it is really quite straightforward. All you need are a few hours, a calculator and the will to do it.

This chapter covers the basics on wholesale suppliers, costing and setting prices. Here are the three most important concepts in this chapter:

1. Buy all your supplies at wholesale prices

2. Calculate all your supply, labor and overhead costs

3. Add profit %, wholesale margins and retail pricing onto your products.

BUYING WHOLESALE

If you remember one thing from this chapter, it is to always buy your supplies at wholesale. Wholesale prices are significantly lower than what you'd pay at retail, which basically means you increase your likelihood of making a profit. If you pay retail prices for your supplies, it will be difficult to make any profit while still selling at prices customers are wiling to pay.

A wholesaler is a business that sells goods to manufacturers or retailers at prices much lower than you'd find at a retail store. You may feel that your business is too small to even approach a large wholesaler, but that is often not true. The only barrier you may face is a minimum order policy. Some operate "cash and carry" warehouses very similar to places like Costco. You go there, pick out what you need from an open warehouse and pay for it on the way out. They will likely need some kind of proof that you are a "real" business so be prepared to show them a business registration number or ask them what they require.

Ordering wholesale supplies is really no different than ordering from a clothing catalogue. Here are a few things to keep in mind:

- Do your own pickups from suppliers if at all possible. Some companies provide free shipping for minimum orders. If product is being shipped to your home, make sure the shipper's truck has a tailgate and pallet jack if you are ordering a whole pallet/skid worth of supplies. Otherwise the driver has to unload boxes by hand.

- Get accounts with your postal service, shipping and courier services. Ask them for their rates and how to save the most money when you are shipping. Bus companies often have shipping services also.

- Buy supplies together with other vendors who use the same supplier. This requires some coordination, but can save you shipping costs if you do not need enough supplies to qualify for free shipping or to even order product. Many companies have minimum orders regardless of their shipping policies.

- Search the yellow pages, Internet, backs of magazines and ask other vendors or retailers where to find wholesale suppliers. Look for suppliers through manufacturing associations, and even check out online resale sites like E-Bay or Craig's List for supplies or equipment.

- Be cautious of "wholesale to the public" stores like Costco. Many of them have great deals, but not always. Do your homework and always comparison shop. Make certain that you check the best before or expiry dates on items if applicable. There is no sense in ordering a vast quantity of supplies if you'll never use it up before its expiry.

- If you need fresh ingredients try to get them from local farmers. Find out from your public health office what an "Approved Source" means and whether or not your farmers qualify. Otherwise, find food suppliers in the yellow pages or look for delivery trucks outside local restaurants to see who delivers in your area.

- Ask for an order number and tracking or waybill numbers so you have a way to track a shipment should it get delayed or lost.

- Do not buy too many supplies at one time. Order only enough for about a three-month period. It is easy to get carried away when looking at catalogues.

- Have *all* the supplies you need in your possession prior to setting a production date. Ask suppliers to inform you *prior* to shipping if they are out of stock on anything you've ordered. This way you can order from someone else and still get supplies in time for your production schedule.

- Always have alternative suppliers in case your main supplier is out of stock.

- Credit terms are when companies allow you to pay for supplies after you've received them. Fill out a credit application and the wholesaler will inform you whether or not they'll give you credit terms. Many companies require you to pay up front for supplies for a period of time, after which you can ask for terms. Some companies allow you to pay by credit card if you pay up front, but will only accept checks or cash if you pay at the end of your credit term date. Check this policy ahead of time so you are not caught short of cash when it comes time to pay your bill.

SUPPLY, LABOR AND OVERHEAD COSTS

Here is a basic chart outlining how to breakdown the costs associated with making a product. There are certainly more complex and perhaps more detailed methods of calculating costs but this should get you well on your way.

Supply Costs	This is the total of all the costs for supplies used in making a product. List only the supplies that go *directly* into the making of the product. For example, in strawberry jam it's berries, sugar, pectin, a jar, lid and label.	1) Calculate the cost of each supply or amount of ingredients used and total the amount per batch, run or unit. 2) Divide the total cost of supplies by the total number of items made during one production run or batch. When making food items like jam, it's easier to calculate ingredient costs by weight and more accurate than measuring by the cup or teaspoon. 3) Add in the cost of any packaging materials and labels.
Direct Labor Costs	The # of hours you put into making the product. It can include set up and clean up time as well. The more product you make at one time means less set up and clean up costs per unit.	1) Time your production from start to finish. 2) Multiply that time by an hourly wage you think is fair to pay yourself. 3) Divide the total labor cost into the total number of items you make during one production run.

Over-head or Indirect Costs	These are all the other business expenses you pay for that do not go directly into the product: rent, gas, utilities, insurance, bookkeeping fees are all examples of overhead. These are also called fixed costs.	1) Total or estimate all your overhead expenses for a year. Divide the total into either the number of hours you worked on your products over a year and add this amount to each product. or 2) Divide the total overhead costs by the # of products you made in a year and add *that* amount to each product. or 3) Estimate a % that might work and add that amount to each item made in one year. You will likely have to reevaluate overhead costs once you have some experience.
Profit	The % added to the total of Supply +Direct Labor + Overhead so that your business makes a profit.	You decide how much profit on top of costs you want to make. Add a % you feel comfortable with 2%, 5%, 10% it's up to you. Most businesses pump profits back into the business for future expansion, better equipment etc.
Cost of Goods Sold (COGS)	This is the total of Supply Costs + Direct Labor + Overhead + Profit Margin	**Add them all up and you have what's known as the COGS, or Cost of Goods Sold.**

ADDING IN THE WHOLESALE MARKUP

Some of you may be asking why you need to add a wholesale price to your product if you are only planning on selling at the markets. This is one of the most frequent questions posed to me by vendors developing their businesses. It is an excellent question and deserves a thorough explanation.

Good products *always* attract retailers who ask if they can buy your products at wholesale to sell in their shops. Customers also frequently ask where they can purchase your products when you are not at the market. While you may very well never have the *intention* of selling at wholesale, if you have well made products that people are buying frequently, you will eventually face this situation.

Wholesaling is an option for spreading the word about your products and leveraging your time by having other people sell them for you. While you may not initially be interested in selling products at wholesale, it is still a good exercise to include this margin into the total cost of your products. This is so you *are* ready if and when you might want to take the next step in your business.

If you choose *not* to build in wholesale pricing, but then eventually want to sell to a retailer, here is what may happen:

Say your Cost of Goods Sold is $5.00 and your market retail price is $7.00. Retailers expect to pay a *wholesale* price up to 50% off your retail price or in this case $3.50 per unit. If the product *costs* you $5.00 to make you're losing money on the deal. If a retailer buys your product at $7.00 they will have to put their own retail price up much higher than what you sell at the market. No retailer will do that. If you are selling your product for $7.00, how can a retailer possibly expect to compete against you?

Then again, if your cost is $5.00/unit and your retail price is $20.00, and the product is selling well at that price point, you've likely given yourself enough room to play with a wholesale price that a retailer can deal with. This takes some time to work through. Do not rush this process because once you set a wholesale price, it is not professional to change your pricing frequently if you've made mistakes. You are better off to spend the time initially to figure out what the best wholesale price should be and then only change it periodically, say, once or twice a year with at least a month or two's notice given to your retailers.

CALCULATING THE WHOLESALE AND RETAIL PRICING

Wholesale pricing	The % or dollar amount added to the cost of goods sold so that you can sell your product at wholesale.	**Formula: Usually done as a % on top of COGS. It varies depending on what your product is.**
Retail pricing	The % you add to the wholesale price that will be the final price a customer pays for your item	**Formula: % added to Wholesale** 100% or more for retail 25-40% for grocery Market pricing, which is what the market will bear.

Retailers assume you have already added in all of the above costs. Do yourself a big favor and build in a wholesale price so you are prepared to sell at wholesale when or if you choose to do so. At the very least, make sure your retail price is high enough so that if you should decide to sell at wholesale sometime in the future, you can work backwards to see if you've got enough room in your margins to still make some profit on top of costs.

If you follow the previous steps in calculating all of your costs, you will come up with a more accurate picture of how much your products really need to sell for if you are to make any kind of profit. Simply adding up some of the costs of supplies, avoiding calculating any labor or overhead costs and forgetting to add a wholesale margin will never reflect the true costs of doing business. If you are a seasoned market vendor and have been scratching your head as to why you never seem to come out on top of the game, you may want to take another look at this section and sharpen up that pencil.

CALCULATING YOUR PRODUCTION STEPS

Let's now go into the concept of breaking down your production steps so you can maximize efficiency and therefore, profits. The basic concept to know is that the more time you save in production and labor costs, the more money you put in your pocket at the end of the day. If you can increase your production efficiency, you can work down some of your production costs.

Here are some suggestions for increasing efficiency.

- Write down each production step and time yourself as you do it. Practice making several items before you time yourself because the first few will always take longer than after you have some experience. You can also videotape yourself while you are doing production. Can you move tools, lighting, seats, tables or other equipment to make production easier and faster? Can you eliminate any steps without losing quality?

- Increase production speed by creating a little assembly line for your products. Instead of cutting out and sewing only one apron from start to finish, cut out five of them at one time. Sew on *all* of the pockets, then *all* of the ties, and then finally sew *all* of the hems. If you can use the same color thread, you won't have to rethread the machine each time you sew a seam. Divide the total production time between the five aprons for an average production time per apron. Grouping the same activities develops a rhythm that increases production speed. Test out this theory by timing one product from start to finish. Then time yourself making multiples. Compare the results and decide which works better.

- Weigh ingredients or supplies whenever possible because weighing is more accurate and consistent from batch to batch. Most food or cosmetic ingredients are sold by weight making them easier to cost than if you did it by the cup or teaspoon. A small kitchen scale is all most people need to get started, but you can find a commercial scale on used goods websites like Craig's List. Just be sure to take someone with you and test the equipment before you buy it and get a sales receipt. Used items rarely, if ever, come with a guarantee. Weighing ingredients often saves time as you do not have to eyeball levels in measuring cups. It also ensures greater accuracy in recipes and reduces the chances of costly mistakes.

Make templates, jigs, patterns and forms for as many tasks as possible that require them. If you are using flimsy paper patterns for your baby bibs, then cut patterns out of heavy cardstock, use weights to hold them down onto several layers of fabric, and use a rotary cutter to cut through the layers all at one time. If you are making wire earrings, use a jig for wrapping the wire so they are the same each time. All of these tasks, while initially take some time to create, will help you reduce production time and save money over multiple units.

Try to eliminate as many repetitive motions as you can, reducing your efforts into the most efficient use of your tools and body as you can. For example, when I fill and cap my mustard jars, I place them directly back into their boxes instead of on a table. This means I don't then have to pick them back up again to place them into the boxes. While this might sound minor, if I multiply each additional movement by the 700 or so jars I make at one time, it quickly adds up in labor costs.

Avoid unnecessary distractions while you work. Cut out any activities that are not directly related to production. Multi-tasking while trying to do a production run will never give you an accurate picture of your time and production costs. Avoid texting your friends while stirring the pot, so to speak.

CONCLUSION

Finding wholesale suppliers and adequately costing and pricing your work is essential to running a business that will make you a profit. The initial investment of time and effort in doing so will save you a lot of headache later on and allow you to transition smoothly into wholesale if you so choose.

Packaging

$\mathscr{P}$ackaging is one of the most important choices you'll make when deciding how to present your products to the public. Packaging can make or break a sale, but it can be expensive, often costing more than the product itself.

Investing in excellent packaging and labeling will make a huge difference in how your products are perceived by customers. Packaging does sells the products, and unless you are the best salesperson in the world, you are likely going to need a solid combination of excellence in product, effective signage, honed sales skills, and knockout packaging.

That's not to say that simple packaging isn't effective. However, if you are going to the effort of making a beautiful product only to package it into something mundane or careless, don't expect thrilled reactions. Once again, there has to be balance. A poorly made or really average product packaged in a slick looking box may sell the product once but may never foster repeat business. Balancing quality product with beautiful packaging will serve you better than choosing one over the other.

TYPES OF CONTAINERS

So, how do you choose the best possible packaging options? Here are some packaging options to consider.

GLASS

Most people use glass jars or bottles for their jams, sauces, preserves and cosmetic products. Many vendors simply go to the supermarket and buy jars at retail prices. If you read the chapter on costing you'll know that buying supplies at retail reduces profits and may make products too expensive to sell at competitive pricing. You can find old jars at thrift stores, but be certain there are no chips or cracks as old jars can break while processing. Once your business starts growing though, it is a good idea to buy glass wholesale.

Do a search online for glass jar manufacturers. Richard's Packaging is a popular company selling all across North America. If you are looking for fancier jars, the Italian company Bruni Glass makes jars and bottles with beautiful shapes, but these are much more expensive than the standard shapes and sizes offered by more conventional companies. If there are other vendors using standard bottles or jars, ask them if they'd be interested in bulk buying. You will get a much better deal if you share a full pallet load of glass than if you each bought fewer cases of jars on your own.

Most of the time, vendors buy glass through a sales rep who may have exclusive rights to sell that product within a given geographic location. If you call the glass company directly, they'll usually give you the number of their broker or sales rep in your area.

Tips on choosing glass jars or bottles.

- It is wise to use stock jars and lids, and then invest in exceptional label design and materials. "Stock" means standard sizes which are always available through the supplier. You will not usually have to worry about the supplier running out or having to wait up to six months for more to arrive from their factories in China. Ask the supplier how long it takes them to ship an order. Make sure you have all your jars or bottles well in advance of production.

- Caps and lids usually cost extra and come in standard colors, often white or gold. If you are looking for any other color, it would have to be specially ordered and will cost more. If you buy a few cases of jars or bottles at a time, buy the same number of lids or caps plus a few extra. As you buy larger quantities of jars, it is easier just to buy an entire box of lids. I always like to buy a few more lids than I think I'll need in case some of the lids fail during production.

- The wind can pick up suddenly at markets so it is crucial to protect your products. While tall ice wine style bottles are beautiful, they are also very expensive and tip over easily. Display all glass bottles in tall-sided baskets to stop them from falling over and crashing on the ground.

- Most glass comes inside shipping boxes, but if you buy an entire skid of jars, they may come loose. If so you may need to buy shipping boxes so you can carry them to and from the market or if you decide to sell wholesale. Ask about this prior to ordering. Avoid paying for custom made boxes until you're absolutely certain that the bottle or jar you're using is the one you want. I made the mistake of having 1000 boxes and 6000 labels made for bottles I no longer use and that no longer fit the bottles I currently use. It was a huge waste of money and every day I see them I am reminded of this mistake. Hopefully sharing these tips with you will help you avoid some of the more unfortunate mistakes I've made.

- Consider jar and bottle sizes carefully. Using a really large jar will mean that it'll take a long time for a customer to finish what is inside. The product may end up going bad before they've used it all up. Look at various sizes of product in grocery stores to see what is typical for your type of product.

- Do not choose too many sizes. A sample size and a standard retail size would be sufficient for most vendors. While small, medium and large sounds like a good idea, it creates too much choice, takes customers too long to decide, and ends up costing you too much in stock and labels if you need different size lids and labels for each jar. Stick to fewer choices, small and big.

- Choose jars or bottles that are easy to label. Flat sided barrel shaped jars and bottles offer more surface area for labeling than hexagonal jars. If you are considering expansion into wholesale, you'll want to pick glass that will go through an automatic labeler. Ask the supplier. Fancy, unusually shaped glass containers are beautiful, but can be difficult to label.

- Heat shrink safety seals are commonly used to prevent customers from opening jars in stores. While not strictly necessary at the markets, consider them if you ever plan on selling wholesale or if your products are not heat processed or sealed. You usually get them custom made to fit your jar or bottle, and put them on using a heat gun.

- Most glass companies will send you samples so you can weigh them, fill a few to see what the product looks like inside, and apply label mockups.

PLASTIC

There are different kinds of plastics used for food, chemical and cosmetics that are not heat processed. Plastic jars are often used for cosmetics as well as dry bath salts. Some plastics have a crystal clear hard quality that sparkles and has a much higher end look than cheaper plastics. Make certain that the plastic you choose is food grade if you'll be putting food into them. The advantage of plastic is that the lighter weight makes for cheaper shipping costs and is easier on the back when you are loading and unloading your vehicle several times a week during market season. It is also less prone to shattering.

POUCHES

Pouches are gaining momentum for many reasons. They are lightweight and non-breakable. They come in different materials like silky Mylar, rice paper, plastic, foil lined and recycled papers. Some can be re-sealed and others have one way gas valves like coffee bags. Some have gusseted bottoms so they stand up on a shelf or table and you can get them with one clear side so you can see the product inside. Punch a hole into the top and hang them on a rack to keep them at eye level, or use vertical racks that have clips on them so you can attach the pouches to the racks. Pouches provide a lot of surface area for labeling and come in many sizes.

Pouches can be used for cookies, snacks, spice mixes, cleaning powders, bath salts, soup mixes, dried fruits, nuts; you name it. Some have spouts on them so they can hold ketchup and BBQ sauces, but the filling machine costs a fortune. Buy plain pouches and apply labels by hand. The pouches can be sealed by what is known as an Impulse Sealer, which you can buy through packaging supply stores.

79

BAGS

Bags can be plastic, paper or fabric, plain, patterned or custom printed. They can be strictly utilitarian or part of a slick marketing plan. Whatever your reasons for using bags, keep in mind the following ideas.

SHOPPING BAGS

While many customers now bring their own shopping bags, it is a good idea to keep some inexpensive plastic bags in your stall. You may want to have bags custom printed with your company name or buy simple rope handled paper bags and wrap your products in colorful tissue paper. Some packaging companies have beautiful bags made from a variety of sensual materials that can really highlight your products. It is true that using plastic bags has become unfashionable. However, the fact remains that at every market, customers still ask for bags. Unless your market forbids the use of new plastic bags, it is up to you to decide whether or not to supply them.

SMALL, FLAT, PAPER BAGS OR LUNCH BAGS

Small paper bags are a good option for putting small items in to carry. Try to find printed bags that represent your image. Have small stickers made with your logo or company name printed on them and use them to seal the bags shut. It is a nice touch.

Roll down the edges of the paper lunch bags and use them instead of expensive paper baskets to hold your pre-weighed fresh produce like potatoes, cherry tomatoes and plums.

PRINTED SHOPPING BAGS

Another possibility is to get bags printed with your company name. It is cheapest to use a single color printing process and many bag companies offer this service. The more you buy, the cheaper each bag costs. Use a color combination that is high contrast so you can see the image from a distance. Reusable shopping bags, paper or plastic bags can all be printed. Some people even create their own designs on stock bags using stencils or stamps, but of course, this takes time and effort.

CELLO BAGS

These bags come in a glossy, crisp material that crinkles and crackles and is reminiscent of opening a gift. Cheaper plastic bags have little to no sensuality. Cello bags come in numerous shapes and sizes, from cones, to flat bags, to those with gussets or cardboard bottoms so they can stand up on shelves. Food grade bags can hold stacks of cookies, small candies, sets of small jars for little gift packs, cookie mixes and any number of other things. They are perfect for gift giving and come in clear or many different printed versions. Dress them up with colorful curling ribbon and change the ribbon color depending on the season. Avoid buying large amounts of decidedly seasonal bags because you will always have leftovers and seasonal bags look strange at other times of the year when they are not relevant. Choose neutral prints like dots, stripes or stars and then dress up the bags with a variety of seasonally colored curling ribbon.

BOXES

Boxes come in an array of shapes, sizes and materials, just like bags. If you are a baker, the standard, thin cardboard boxes that fold up can be taped with your logo sticker to keep shut. Tie on some lovely curling ribbon and you will have a sleek and polished look. Paper produce boxes are generally in standard sizes or pints, quarts etc. and are usually green but other colors are available. Produce placed in these containers looks tidier than a huge pile of beans heaped loosely onto a table and keeps delicate or round produce from rolling off the table. Many vendors simply put the produce into plastic produce bags and reuse the boxes.

PLASTIC PRODUCE BAGS

These come on a roll and are inexpensive. Many fresh produce vendors find that pre- weighing and bagging produce is better than allowing customers to pick through large bins. If you pre-bag your items, customers can't pick through items or damage produce. They can easily pick up what they need, and it's visually tidier. It also increases the speed of transactions, which is key when you're running a busy produce stand with long customer lines.

Experiment with a variety of display styles and you'll quickly see what your customers respond well to. Play around with different kinds of bags and either open stock or pre-bagged items.

CONCLUSION

Everything you do reflects on your approach to business and contributes to the impression your customers have of you, and the quality and value of your products. From the product to stall design, packaging to labels, your dress and your attitude, it all tells customers and other vendors how seriously you take your business. It does not have to be fancy, but it should clearly identify you, your style and your products.

Remember, too, that customers may be buying your products as a gift for others. Their choice to buy from you is a reflection on *them*, on their taste and on how much they value the recipient of that gift. Look for packaging options that are simple, easily labeled, clean, and display a cohesive image.

The next chapter gets into more details on design for both food and craft vendors.

Design

$\mathcal{F}$irst impressions are critical in a busy open market where people will either be attracted to your stall or walk by without a second glance. Whether you are selling eggplants or candles, applying some basic design principles will make the market environment more enjoyable for everyone.

Presenting a professional and attractive business image at the markets reassures customers that they can trust you and your products. However, instead of stalls and labels that wow customers, the norm seems to range from lackluster to downright boring. Effective design is inviting, welcoming and inspiring. It encourages interaction between customers and vendors. Good design nurtures a healthy sales environment.

Design is, simply, the appearance of everything in your business: the color and shape of your products; the way they are arranged on the table, your banners, labels, business cards, and signs. It is the way you dress, your hairstyle, and how you present yourself to the public. It all is a reflection of your personality. It also manifests in how you approach a sales transaction, and how the traffic flows in and around your stall.

These are the basic steps to consider when approaching the concept of design:

Decide how you want customers to feel about you, your stall and your products.

Pick colors and designs that support the feeling you want customers to have.

Create signs, labels and marketing materials that fit the image.

Have banners, labels and signs made, and buy or build displays.

Evaluate how it all works together and make changes as needed.

CREATING A DESIGN STYLE

The first step in deciding on a design approach is knowing how you want your customers to feel when they first see your stall. Do you want them to laugh heartily at your displays? Do you want them to rub their tummies and rush over to buy one of your cinnamon buns? Do you want them to feel enveloped by deep rich, sensual color, or feel uplifted and clean in a soft white environment? Colors, shapes, and textures are evocative and visceral but often subtle and unconsciously experienced. We've all had experiences of feeling wonderful in certain environments and cold and uncomfortable in others. Much of this has to do with the design of the environment itself.

Your choices create an emotional and physical impact that will shape a customer's entire experience of your business. You are essentially creating a little store and you want customers to be attracted to you. The main thing to remember is that you want people to *buy* your products, so your design choices should work to enhance your products not overwhelm or distract them for making purchasing decisions.

The next time you go to a local market or even the mall, look closely at which stores draw you in. Which ones attract you and what kind of stores do you avoid? What colors, shapes, smells, sounds and textures appeal to you or repel you? Are soft surfaces appealing to you or do you prefer hard, clean lines? Do you like stores packed with items or spaced out so you can really see individual items easily? What things inspire you to reach out and touch them, and what do you avoid? Observe and you'll get a very good idea of what you like, what you do not.

While some people may scoff at the idea of applying design principles to a market business, I encourage you to experiment and see what works best for you. I also suggest that people go with their gut. If it seems completely foolish to you to create a stall with matching or coordinating colors, then by all means, stick with what you know. If you are satisfied by your sales, and are happy with what you have, then great! There's no reason to keep reading this section.

However, if you're finding that you wished you had better sales, aren't really sure what to do that might improve results, then continue on. Generally speaking, people don't want to say negative things to vendors. If your stall is uninspiring or you're not very welcoming, customers will simply pass you by and go where they feel more inspired to spend their money, knowing full well that the vendor in that booth will likely be nicer to them in the process. It's up to you.

AN INSPIRING DESIGN THEME

If you set up an inspiring stall, your customers will be inspired as well. More than anything else, your attitude will be more important than design any day of the week. Still, if you're not feeling your best, if you're tired or there are things happening in your life that make it really hard to be the super sales person you are usually, then it sure is nice to have a complete package of cohesive display to fall back on.

Take a moment right now to answer the following questions. Do not think too much about it. Just go with the first thing that pops into your head.

What colors are most of your clothes and home decor?

Do you like hard, crisp, geometric lines or soft, fluid organic shapes?

Do you like rich, saturated colors, or muted soft pastel shades?

Are you energetic, lively and talkative, or calm, reserved and quiet? If you can be both, which one gives you more energy and which one is more of an effort?

The answers to the above questions will give you a simple plan for your approach to design. If you usually wear purples and browns and like to wear lime green as an accent color, then there is your color scheme: a brown tablecloth, purple shelves and labels, with lime green signs and banners. Wear a brown and purple market apron and trim it in lime green. Use lime green shopping bags, purple tissue and have business cards made with the same colors. If you like crisp lines, then use crisp, tight fonts for the lettering on your banners and marketing materials. If you like soft, organic fluid lines, then choose those ones, as long as they can be seen from a distance.

It is as simple as that. It will keep the theme cohesive, not confusing. The key here is proportion. Ninety per cent of your color scheme should be the main colors, and the accent should be no more than about 10%. This is just a ballpark figure, not a rule. Avoid using too many colors or the look will be confusing and your products may not stand out. Your products should remain the focus of your stall and your color choices should serve to highlight the products. I would, however, avoid extremely bright colors or neon colors like those found in emergency vests seen on traffic control personnel. Fluorescent colors do, indeed, attract attention and if you're selling doggy raincoats with reflective tape, then fine. But overall, these colors are fatiguing and hurt the eyes after a while. Remember that you are the one who will also have to live with the colors every day, so pick ones that you love and make you feel great.

Once you've chosen some colors and ideas for the general feeling for your stall, it is time to create an effective stall display with a banner, labels, signs, and your business cards and brochures to help support your sales.

BANNERS

A banner is a large, flexible poster with metal grommets that you attach onto the back of your tent or on the front face of your canopy. Good ones are made of vinyl, do not fade, last for years without cracking and are flexible enough to roll up and put in a carrying tube.

It is the most important sign to get for your stall. An effective banner should be easily visible from 20 feet out in front of your stall, and answer two questions:

- Who are you?
- What are you selling?

Here are two examples of easy to read banners

If you have many different products, or products that change depending on the season, it is best to make a banner that is neutral. Choose a company name that represents what you sell. Mountain Farm Produce is a good example. Mention the name of the farm, the fact that you sell produce and that is all that needs to go on the banner. Avoid naming individual products, like *"We sell beans and eggs"* on a banner if you ever plan on creating more products in the future. A better option would be *"We sell beans, eggs and more!"*

Given that banners can be expensive, you want your banner to remain relevant as long as possible. If you know you are only ever going to sell one product, then certainly design a banner to highlight this fact. If you are the "pickle man" a simple bright green sign printed with *PICKLE MAN* and a clear graphic of a pickle is all you need. However if you are a farm stall specializing in certified organic, biodynamic produce, then say as much: *ABC Farms -Certified Organic Biodynamic Produce.*

MAKING A BANNER

A homemade banner can add an artsy or rustic feel to your stall that can certainly work to enhance your image. However, they can also look cheap and might not be readily seen from a distance. Some paints can run or fade. Homemade banners may also tear, wrinkle, and otherwise look weather beaten after only a season or two. Still they can be a good option when you're first starting out.

Listed below are several options for creating inexpensive banners.

- Use rigid corrugated plastic board available at office supply or art supply stores and then glue or paint letters on the surface. You can buy a small grommet application tool at fabric shops so that you'll be able to suspend these rigid signs with bungee cords. This is one of the least expensive ways of creating a sign. Treat these signs with care as they easily dent and crease.

- Use a paint drop cloth or buy some heavy canvas from an art supply store. Fold over the edges and glue them down so they do not fray. Paint both sides of the canvas with latex primer, or a common art primer called gesso. Let it dry and then paint on your main color and company name. Lots of paint stores sell small tubs of sample latex paint. This is a less expensive way of buying paint than going to an art supply store. Use several coats of varnish and then attach grommets to the corners so you can hang it up. This can work well until you can afford to have a banner made, but be careful not to fold it as it will easily crack and crease.

- Use painted planks of wood or plywood with eyebolts screwed into the corners so they can be suspended. This works well for craft made from natural materials and of course for farm produce because it has a rustic look. Make sure they are well attached and in no danger of falling.

- Buy a large picture frame from a thrift shop, paint the frame in one of your colors, make your sign from canvas or even a thin piece of plywood, and staple it to the back of the frame. Suspend it using eyebolts screwed into the top corners. Avoid using easels in your booth because they fall over in the wind and are trip hazards.

- Make a fabric sign. Some people quilt, appliqué or otherwise embellish a soft piece of fabric that hangs in the stall. It is a nice touch that may be in keeping with the theme of your stall. Use sturdy, weatherproof fabrics if you can so the sign does not get damaged in the rain, but realize that most fabrics will fade in strong sunlight. Make sure the words are easily visible from a distance.

PROFESSIONAL BANNERS AND SIGNS

If you have some money to invest, find a local sign shop and ask them to make you a banner. Sign shops usually have someone there to help you with your ideas and can create several versions on the computer to help you decide. They also have access to high quality UV rated inks and can apply grommets to the edges and make sure to ask if they fold the edges over. Some banners have straight cut edges that tend to curl over time. They will likely charge you for some design time so weigh out the costs with the time you'd spend making your own sign and decide whether it is worth the investment.

It was a good investment for me. I had my banner made in 2004, and it is still in excellent shape today six years later. Check out companies like www.vistaprint.com for all kinds of deals on inexpensive sign and marketing support materials.

Avoid buying too much stuff at first and do not get sucked into spending money on give away items like pencils or key chains. Customers are happy to take them, but usually end up throwing them away later.

LABELS

Customers looking for a special gift may be more inclined to buy something from a vendor who has taken the time to create attractive, well made labels.

Giving a shoddy looking gift is always a reflection on what the gift-giver thinks of the recipient.

Creating simple, attractive, professional looking labels is not difficult and does not have to cost a lot. There is inexpensive label making software available at many office and computer stores. The Print Shop is one example. They have templates to use that match stock labels from Staples or Avery.

Labels can make or break a product. Sloppy, handwritten, crooked labels applied with a glue stick do not convey a professional or trustworthy image. If the label is bad, what does that say about the resulting quality of the product inside the packaging?

Simple, beautiful display

Next time you go into a gourmet food shop or the supermarket, take a close look at labels you really like. What attracted your eye? Was it the colors, the texture of the label material itself, the images, typeface and size of the fonts? Can you tell from a distance what the product is? Is the name of the product easily visible on the front of the label? How many labels are there on a package? More labels mean more labor costs. Take a look at labels that evoke little to no reaction in you and ask yourself why that is.

If you are creating food products, be aware that there are labeling laws you may have to consider. Both the Canadian Food Inspection Agency (CFIA) and the American Food and Drug Administration (FDA) have labeling laws on their websites.

http://www.inspection.gc.ca/english/fssa/labeti/labetie.shtml

http://www.fda.gov/Food/LabelingNutrition/default.htm

Fortunately, food labeling requirements for selling at the markets are usually more relaxed than when you sell wholesale to stores. At the very least you will need a list of ingredients, the volume or weight and your company name and contact information. You may also need nutritional data. Read the labeling laws and contact agents at the CFIA or FDA for more information. If you are selling value-added food items, it is also important to include lot numbers and expiry or best before dates so you can accurately track back your production to specific dates and ingredient lot numbers should the need arise.

With crafts items, any hang tags, labels, flyers, or brochures that detail specific care instructions should be included with the sale of each product, especially if they are purchased as a gift.

PRINTING LABELS

The easiest and least expensive thing to do is to buy stock labels from Staples or other office supplies stores and print them yourself on a color laser copier. Create a simple label, print out a test sheet on plain paper, cut it out and tape it to your packaging so you can see what it looks like. Once you've decided on a label design, then print them out on the stock labels and apply them to the packaging. Do not use ink jet printers as the inks run in damp or rainy weather. Take advantage of periodic sales on color laser printing or copying at your local print shop or office supply store.

Once you are printing several hundred labels at one time, it may be cheaper to approach a small print shop and ask them to print off some labels for you. I do not recommend buying your own color printer or copier because the inks are very expensive and home printers or copiers are not designed for large numbers of copies.

Once your business grows to the point that you are selling thousands of products a year, you may want to have a commercial printer do the labels for you. There are a variety of options on having labels printed commercially.

BAR CODES/ UPC (UNIVERSAL PRODUCT CODE)

People frequently ask whether or not they need to get bar codes for their value-added food products. The short answer is no, not if you are only selling at the markets.

You only need barcodes when you start wholesaling your products to large grocery or chain stores. Most market vendors who expand into the wholesale market sell to small stores that may not use a scanning system.

A barcode is an electronic tracking system that identifies your company and products. When a vendor wholesales to a large store, inventory clerks enter your barcode into their system and assign a price for that product. When someone buys the product, the checkout clerk scans the product and the computer system applies the cost to that customer's bill. The store does not have to put a price tag on each product and their system automatically knows that one of the products was sold. The barcode system is linked to inventory so the store's buyers know when to replenish their stock.

If you do want barcodes there are two ways to get them. You can "rent" codes from a large distributor like GS-1. http://www.gs1.org/ They offer a variety of services, charge initiation and yearly fees. It is expensive and usually meant for large companies with thousands of products. You can also just buy a code online from a company like www.simplybarcodes.net. It is legal, there are no initiation or yearly fees and the more codes you buy at once, the cheaper they are. You also own the code forever. If you discontinue a product, wait until all the current stock is sold out of the marketplace and then recycle the code to use on another product.

The only thing I would avoid doing is making up your own number and then putting it on a product. There is barcode software that can do this for you, but you will never know if the number you choose is legitimately being used by another company.

BUSINESS ACCESSORIES AND PROMOTION

There are several ways to create an identity for your business. Having a printer create advertising that can be handed out is an ideal way to promote both you and your products. You need to decide which would be the most effective way to tell people about your business.

BUSINESS CARDS

Vendors have mixed feelings about business cards. Some believe that it is an essential marketing tool that allows customers or potential customers a chance to remember you after visiting the market. Other people believe that when a customer asks for a card, you've lost a sale. Customers often ask for a card as a way of bowing out gracefully, but what it might mean is this: *"I have no intention of buying anything but will you give me something for free anyway?"* This creates an illusion that they are interested in your business and may come back sometime later. It's kind of like saying, " hey, let's do lunch sometime" to someone you really couldn't care less about seeing again.

Instead of just handing out cards, why not create cards that serve another function as well. Create cards you punch or initial, offering customers a discount or free product once they've bought a set number of your products. This is what many coffee shops do. You could give a discount (if you can afford it!) when they bring the card back with them to the market. This encourages customers to *keep* the card instead of throwing it in the recycling bin as soon as they get home. Think more creatively about the standard business card and you might come up with some other ideas that will provide greater benefits to you and your customers than simply handing out a card with your name on it.

Whatever you decide, consider carefully the benefits you get from spending money on some kind of marketing tool. Do not get cards made just because that is what everyone else does. In my view, if someone does not have the cash to buy a jar of my mustard after sampling and enjoying it, then a card is not likely going to entice them to buy it later. They either like it, need it, and can afford it, or they do not really want it. It may be totally different for someone who sells a different product so try it out, evaluate the response and see if cards really do result in people coming back or calling you with orders later.

BROCHURES AND FLYERS

Flyers and brochures are used to educate and inform. Recipes, company history, processing descriptions, usage or care instructions and price lists are all commonly put in brochures. Brochures explain your services or business specifics. If you do not have the time to explain what biodynamic farming is, put it in a brochure and hand it out to customers for them to read later. If you sell a variety of apples, a brochure can help identify them. A photo of each apple, general date of availability, description and serving suggestions all help customers learn about the different varieties. Many market vendors have to educate customers about the benefits of their products, but may not have the time to get into the details while they are busy selling on market day. Brochures or flyers allow them to pass along this information for customers to absorb later on and allows the vendor to focus on sales.

There is design software available to create your own brochures and many people use programs like Microsoft Publisher to create their own.

WEBSITES, BLOGS AND SOCIAL NETWORKING

Today's love affair will all things electronic has many vendors asking me about whether or not they should construct a website, keep a blog or use social networking to connect with customers outside of market hours. All I can say is that you need to weigh the costs of your time as compared to the return on investment in terms of sales or public education. I caution you that it's worse to start onto this road and neglect it if you find that you don't have the time, than not going there at all. Are you getting into a market business so you can have more freedom and time to yourself? If so, then it might be a good idea to ask yourself whether or not these kinds of activities will serve to enhance that part of your life, or simply clutter it up. Websites do have their uses, especially if you plan on doing some online sales or have recipes or information that might be useful to your customers. Just be certain you can maintain the site and keep it up to date.

COMMERCIAL PRINTING

As your business grows, you may want to take advantage of the services provided by large commercial printing operations. Once you've developed a line of products and find that it is taking you a lot of time to get labels and brochures printed, you may want to get a quote from a commercial printing house that can actually save you money and time. You must also remember that commercial printing does take some time, so you have to plan ahead. Do not wait until a day or two before you need the labels to place an order. You will need a few weeks' lead-time depending on the printer and what you need to have done. Here are a number of terms and printing specifics that will give you an idea of what to look for when searching for a commercial printer.

DIGITAL PRINTING

Digital printing offers savings for runs under 10,000 units. A computer graphic file is fed directly into the printing machine and the labels are printed off all at once using a dry ink toner cartridge. The process is similar to a color photocopier, but on a much larger scale. This is how I get all of my labels printed and it's served me well for years. The advantage of this is in how you configure the number of labels you need. If you have ten different jams and want 2,000 labels, you do not have to divide up the run equally between the ten labels. You can print 400 labels of one variety of jam, 50 of another and 800 of another, etc. You can divide up the run to whatever quantity of each label you need as long as they are all the same size. The disadvantage of this printing system is that if you only want to print *one* type of label after the initial run, you will pay more than if you printed off all ten labels on that file. One advantage is that if you decide to change the label, all you have to do is pay the designer to make the changes and there is usually a nominal file change fee applied to the next run of labels done.

OFFSET PRINTING

Offset printing presses separate each color onto specially made metal plates and each color is run through separately. The process uses wet inks and takes longer to dry than digital processing. You have to get printing plates made and they can be really expensive. If you make any changes to the label, you have to get new plates made. This type of printing process really only makes financial sense if you are running more than 10,000 units at a time and is not usually appropriate for small market businesses.

HIRING A GRAPHIC DESIGNER

If you have the money, but lack computer or design skills, hiring a graphic designer to create your labels, brochures and business cards is an option to consider, especially if you are planning on moving into wholesale markets. Graphic designers either work independently, for design firms, or commercial printers. A designer should give you a full quote for their services and some will manage the printing aspect of it as well. A less expensive option would be to hire a design student from a local college or even hire someone you know who has competent computer design skills. I have worked with a graphic designer since the inception of my business. I have a good design sensibility, but no time to learn computer graphics skills.

Your budget and skills will dictate what you can afford. Sometimes you can hire a designer to do the initial graphic designs for you, and then take the resulting computer files to the copy shop and print them out yourself until you can afford to pay for digital print jobs.

HIRING A PHOTOGRAPHER AND USING IMAGES

Sometimes you need some good photos taken of your products, action shots of you making your products and photos of your displays. This is for promotional brochures, banners, and cards as well as application forms for markets, large craft fairs or Christmas fairs. Be sure to check with the photographer on whether or not you will own the rights to the photos after they have been taken. Some photographers have a separate price if you want to own the photographs outright. Some, however, will retain the rights to the photographs and you have to "rent" the image each and every time you want to use it in your promotional materials. I have always purchased the rights to my photographs and am glad I did so because now I can use them whenever and however I want.

This also goes for graphic design services and label design. Always ask for specifics in writing so there is no question as to your rights to any images you have made for you.

Another option for using photos is to go to online photo resources and rent or buy images, or download free share images that you can use at will. Sites like www.istockphotos.com have lots of images you can buy, download and use. It's often the cheaper way to go if you need a specific image than hiring a photographer.

HIRING FRIENDS AND FAMILY

Think very carefully about the pros and cons of asking a friend or family member to do design work for you. I hear more stories about failed promises, poor design results and strained relationships than about excellence and commitment. Imagine having to tell a family member that the work they did is not acceptable. Be certain you have complete faith in their abilities and commitment. Let them know that if you are not happy with the work, or if it is not done by the deadline, you'll have to look elsewhere. Still, if someone you know is talented and trying to create a portfolio then that might be a good option.

Make expectations and timelines very clear and write up an agreement so both parties are clear on expectations. This is something you should do in any kind of professional relationship.

CONCLUSION

If you are interested in developing a thriving business, a cohesive, integrated design approach shows your dedication, professionalism and style.

While some vendors can get away with lackluster stall displays if they have high demand products or exceptional sales skills, most of us have to put in a bit more effort to make a sale.

Have fun with this part of the process and understand that you will most likely go through an evolution of design options as you progress with your market business. It may take you a while to find a design concept that really works for you, but you'll get there.

Golda's Finest Foods Pesto

Fresh, local apples

Stalls and Displays

$\mathcal{T}$he image you portray through your products, packaging, display, personal appearance and hygiene all contribute to a customer's perception of the quality of your products.

Unfortunately, for every vendor who creates a lovely stall, I see others whose stalls do not reflect the care and attention they've obviously put into their products. A stall need not be complicated or fancy, but it should be designed to work best for your products and level of sales skill. If you've created products people need and want, then a simple, well-designed stall coupled with a personable and attentive attitude is all you need. While some vendors do well on the sheer force of their personalities and sales skills, most of us benefit from taking at least some basic steps to create a clean, organized and efficient stall. This chapter will help you sort out the various possibilities of stall and display design so you can better promote your wares.

STALL LAYOUT

A standard stall usually consists of a 10' x 10' space, with one or more access points. If your stall is situated in a line with vendors on either side of you, your customers will have access to only one 10' width if your table is placed straight across the front of the stall. Sometimes you may get placed on a corner and have two sides from which to sell. This can be beneficial if you have lots of products and more than one person working with you in the stall.

SINGLE FRONTAGE

For a 10' x 10' space, most vendors have one table (or two tables placed side by side in a single line). They cover it with a cloth and then place items on top, usually with some kind of display shelf.

Be wary of buying really large tables as they are heavy, awkward to move and difficult to load into and out of vehicles. The trick is to design the stall for the best possible display of your products, but one that will allow you to easily and safely monitor your products to avoid any possibility of theft.

For the single vendor, however, two or more sides may be problematic given your limited ability to see what is happening on all sides at once. At first you will tend to change your display frequently as you see what works and what does not.

If you are tall, like me, then you really need to create height so you do not kill your back bending over your wares all day long. I built two 4' x 2' tables out of a standard sheet of ¾ inch plywood and attached metal folding legs to the bottoms. These tables have received some rough treatment over the last six years but have held up well and at a minimum cost. They also fit easily into the back of my truck and I can lift them myself with no problems. I can also separate them to create two tasting stations with a pay table between them for the busy Christmas Fairs.

I also have a small, plastic, folding table for my cash box and supplies, while a small wooden TV table holds my hand washing station. That is it. I've been successfully using this set up for six years. It is quick and easy to set up, break down, and load.

The advantages of this set up are numerous. There is only one direction from which customers can approach my stall so I am always able to attend to customers as they arrive. I have ample room in my stall to store stock, and I can put personal items out of view and under the tables. I can easily manage my entire table and no one can go around where I cannot see what they are doing.

The only real disadvantage of this kind of set up is if you have bulky items like bushy plants and hanging baskets, or many different kinds of produce that need more space than a single table across the front of the stall. There are other designs that work better for those kinds of things.

As you can see in the photo below, this new vendor has successfully integrated her products' Scottish origins with her banner, tablecloth and even her skirt! This is her first year at the market, but her display shows careful thought and simple, clean design. Most importantly, she greets customers with a warm, welcoming smile.

Single frontage stall with an integtrated theme

U-SHAPED SET-UP

Some vendors prefer to have an open looking stall and place tables along the sides of the stall (creating a U-shape) allowing customers to come inside the stall. This set up requires more tables, more cloths, and your personal items and extra stock have to be stored underneath the tables. If you erect tent walls along the sides and back, make sure they are well secured so they do not billow out on windy days knocking over your display or that of your neighbor's.

The advantage of this layout is that customers feel free to walk into the stall out of the steady stream of customers out front. They are closer to you physically and you can walk up to customers to give them personal attention. Make sure anything of great value is well secured onto the tables, especially if they are breakable because it is common for customers who carry bags on their shoulders to inadvertently knock over items.

U-shaped stall

CORNER STALLS

If you have lots of product, more than one person to work in the stall or have items that are best viewed from several angles, like plants, you may try to negotiate for a corner stall. This way you have two sides from which to sell. You will need more tables, cloths, display units and some system to keep an eye on customers.

Since it rains frequently where we live, vendors often set their tables well back from the edges of the tent canopies to avoid rain dripping down the necks of their customers or onto their stock.

The stall below is set back from the outside edge of the 10' x 10' space with a small, but organized space in behind for the vendor to keep personal items. This vendor has cleverly created a three-sided table design, added plastic piping onto the legs of the table to increase their height and has display units propped up so they are closer to eye level.

Corner stall

While black is an unusual color for stall draping, it works beautifully here to focus the eye on the display units and the unique stones of her jewelry. The stall is well organized and the jewelry is displayed at a height that makes it easy for customers to see.

The vendor admits to taking one and a half hours to set up, while take down is always faster. You have to judge the benefits of a design like this with your commute time, your ability to set up and take down within the timeline allotted to vendors and, of course, your stamina.

Remember too that every minute you are not directly selling your products is time you are spending on your business for which you make no revenue. Would you rather set up and break down quickly, or create a slow to set up stall that is so attractive that customers flock to you? Only you can decide whether this is worth it to you.

STREET-SIDE STALLS

Many times markets line each side of a street with sidewalks behind the stalls open to the public. Depending on whether there are stores lining the streets, you may or may not be allowed to put up your back tent wall.

I urge caution when you are in markets like this as your focus will be forwards and away from the back of your tent. Be sure to place any personal items inside covered bins or under your tables so you know where they are.

Customers frequently like to walk through the back of the stalls in order to access the market. This can be disconcerting, especially when they trip or knock things over on their way through, which has happened to me many times. To prevent this, put up your back wall if appropriate, and stack large boxes and covered containers along the back of the stall so no one wants to climb over and around them. If it looks untidy, then cover the boxes with a piece of fabric to keep things neat. Another trick is to buy ten-foot long bungee cords from the dollar store and string them at waist or chest height along the back or sides of the tent. This is a visual deterrent and lets customers know they're not supposed to duck under and walk through your tent.

When customers typically have difficulty getting to the market from one direction, mention it to your market coordinators to see if an access alley can be created between a few stalls so this is not an ongoing problem.

EXTENDING BEYOND YOUR STALL'S BOUNDARIES

Stalls typically are 10' x 10' and most markets have a fairly strict rule about staying within the confines of the stall. If your display starts creeping out onto the market area, you risk tripping customers who are looking elsewhere and you block access to your neighbors' stalls.

Another problem for some vendors is when customers create lines that extend sideways right across the entrance of another vendor's stall. This has happened to me on numerous occasions and because I'm not shy, I ask them to move away from my stall so as to allow access for my customers. If you find yourself in this situation, please make sure you stay on top of how lines are developing in front of your stall. Take a look around and make sure customers are not blocking access to other people's stalls.

ATTRACTIVE FIRST IMPRESSIONS

Customers will be attracted to stalls and displays that are warm and inviting. Here are the main things to consider.

- Get the best quality tent and canopy you can afford and practice putting it up a few times before you go to your first market. A shabby old tent says that you are cutting corners, maybe even in the quality of your products.

Caravan makes the best tents around. I prefer the EZ-Up tent because I can put it up by myself. Some market associations offer a bulk-buying discount for vendors. Call the associations early in the spring to see if they are offering a deal. You can also buy them at Costco in the spring, but they often sell out by early summer.

Tents and canopies are essential pieces of equipment for vendors serious about attending several markets a week and you will be thankful if you have one. Avoid tents that have numerous metal poles that you have to sort through and connect. They are notoriously difficult, and when you break down your tent, they make an awful clanging noise as they fall to the ground and roll all over the place. Everyone knows the new vendors on the block by the fact they always seem to initially buy these tents and all you hear is muffled cursing as they try to put it for the very first time. Save yourself the headache and get a good tent. If you decide that market life isn't for you, you'll likely be able to sell it very easily or use it in your garden.

- Create height on your table both to save your back and to bring products up to eye level. Leaving product on a flat surface forces everyone to look down and does not foster eye contact between you and the customer. Some vendors use plastic plumbing pipe for table legs or put blocks of wood under the legs to lift the table higher. Others put boxes or small shelving units on the table. I put two wood boxes on the table and then place a shelf I bought at Home Depot right on top of the boxes.

Here is an example of a custom made display that beautifully highlights the vertical quality of the packaging. Product belong to the Mitchell Soup Co.

- Drape your display tables with tablecloths that go right to the ground. It looks better from the front of the stall and you can put your personal items out of sight and under the table. Search thrift stores for good quality old curtains, tablecloths or sheets in your color scheme, cut them to the right size and finish off the edges.

Cover bare shelves with a coordinating piece of fabric. If you do not sew, fabric stores and places like Walmart carry double-sided iron-on hem tape that works well to finish off the edges. Just fold the edges over, slip the hem tape in between and iron it closed. Try to find materials that do not wrinkle. Scrunch up the material in your hand and if it wrinkles when you release it, look for another material. The clearance bins at fabric stores are another good place to buy inexpensive fabrics.

- Avoid placing products directly on the table if they could roll or fall over and break. Put products into baskets first, and then put them on the table. Thrift stores are a great place to find inexpensive baskets. It is especially important to prevent breakage due to purses or bags swinging around, from dogs who like to sniff the edges of tables, and from small children with curious hands.

- If you sell a food product that needs some kind of consumer education, then cook some recipes using your products and take good photos of the dish. Laminate and display the photos next to each product. Good photos will always attract customers and by providing recipes with each purchase you will have a much better chance of selling the product than if you just told them about a nice recipe.

This is a close up of my booth. The photo of the roasted chicken up top attracts a lot of customers. They all want to know what is on the chicken.

- If you are selling handcrafted items, find photos of similar items being worn by celebrities, or placed in home settings. Do you make fake fur pillows that are currently fashionable? Show framed magazine photos of similar pillows in a beautiful home or mock up your own photos. This technique helps customers imagine these items in their *own* homes.

Why is it that I've never once seen a plant seller showing photos of their plants in a garden setting? If you make patio planters or garden furniture, why not show pictures of them in a real setting? Ask customers to send you photos of your products in their own homes and ask for testimonials that you can display.

Soaps displayed in nice baskets with clear labels

- Create brightly colored product signs that are easy to read from a distance. If you see people squinting, either the signs are not big enough or you've used a font that is difficult to read. Laminate all of your signs so the rain does not damage them. Regular colored paper does fade in the sun so you'll likely have to make new signs every year but it's not expensive to do this. Print out several copies and put them in a file to laminate later on when they need replacing.

- Sandwich boards and easels are notorious trip hazards, and dogs love to pee on them. Some markets forbid their use or do not allow them to stick out beyond the borders of your 10' x 10' stall. They frequently topple over in the wind and lettering can smudge or run in rainy weather. Securely attach signs to your table, shelves or tent legs.

- You can also suspend signs from inside the stall. Punch holes in laminated signs, and string them together with binder rings. This way you can change them depending on what products you have on any given day.

- Duct tape is a vendor's friend. Always keep a roll with you, along with string, scissors and safety pins and even some zap straps.

- If you use a dry erase board or chalk board, make sure your writing is big enough to read from a distance. Make sure to clean the board well so it always looks neat.

- If you sell clothes or some kind of wearable, make sure you have a mirror and a changing room. Hand mirrors work fine for jewelry, but most people need a taller mirror for clothes. Create a secure and stable method for erecting the mirror especially during windy days.

- Create a changing room by partitioning off a back corner of the stall with a cloth strung between the struts. I've even seen vendors suspend a hoola hoop strung with a shower curtain. Thought that was clever.

- Create a sense of abundance. Pile it high, watch it fly, is an old adage that is still relevant today. Keep your stall well stocked at all times.

- If you are selling out, combine baskets or spread items out, and try to fill in spaces with display items. Some vendors bring bales of hay; others might bring buckets, farm tools, toy scarecrows or stuffed animals to pad their displays as they sell out. Do not be surprised though, if customers want to buy your displays!

- The best thing to do, of course, is to bring enough product with you to last the day.

MANAGING YOUR STALL

- Make sure you can comfortably load and unload your vehicle, and set up and break down your tent and stall display BY YOURSELF! If you cannot, then you will always have to rely on someone else's help. Vendors are often helpful, but you really should not rely on them to help you each week. What would happen if they were not there some day? Ask your market board if they could have someone to help you every week if you require assistance.

- Practice setting up your stall and breaking it down several times before you go to your first market. Develop a repeatable system for yourself so it becomes a habitual practice instead of a mad panic each time you set up and break down.

  Remember that the more tables, display shelves, baskets and such you have, the longer it generally takes to set up and break down a stall. I love IKEA's nesting, lightweight shelving units used for holding CDs. There is a box with two shelves inside them. I pull out the shelves, flip them over and use them as risers while putting a wooden shelf on top of the main boxes. At the end of the day, they nest right back up together and make for compact storage.

- Always bring some thin blocks of wood (shims) to keep your table level if your stall is on uneven ground.

- Frequently check that your stall is well stocked and organized. Are the tablecloths even, have any of your signs fallen down, is your stock well displayed, looking full and abundant?

- How about you? Are your hands and nails clean, hair combed, is your oral and personal hygiene at its best? Are you wearing clean clothes? Your appearance is just as important as your stall.

- Keep your canopy, tablecloths, and all your display items clean and in good repair. Make notes of what needs to be fixed in a notebook specifically reserved for the market. Write down what needs to be done, review the notes at the end of the day when you are tallying up your revenues and plan to get tasks done as soon as you can after each market day. Otherwise you'll forget about it until the next time you set up your stall.

- Try out different display ideas. If you see a vendor whose stall you particularly admire, ask if they'd mind giving you some tips for your stall.

- You can never go wrong with **LARGE**, easy to read signs.

WHAT <u>NOT</u> TO DO

Customers will be attracted to stalls and displays that are organized and give a pleasing first impression.

However, just for fun, I took a picture to show you all the things that you should never do. Take a close look at the photo below and make a list of all the things I've done wrong and then check the list below the phtograph to see if there is anything you've missed.

Do I look ready for business to you, or would you just walk by?

Did you find all the things I did wrong? Check below and see how many you spotted.

- Tablecloth is crooked and does not go all the way to the ground.

- Cash box is open on the table and within reach of potential thieves.

- A bottle has fallen over and could roll onto the ground and break.

- I am facing away from the customer and rudely stuffing my face. Vendors should never be eating when they're sampling food items. If you need to eat something, keep it well away from the food service area, eat discreetly and then wash your hands before sampling.

- My coffee cup, cell phone, and personal papers are on the table where they could easily be stolen. Personal items should always be off the table and out of sight.

- There is no cohesive display. Bags are thrown haphazardly on the table, my mustard jars are not lined up neatly and basically, the whole thing looks a mess.

- There are display units, but no signs or banner displaying who I am or what I sell.

[And yes, I messed up my own stall just as an example. I could hardly ask another vendor if I could take a photo of their stall for my book's *What Not to Do* section! Can you imagine?]

CONCLUSION

Your stall should be warm and inviting. Your stall and displays are a reflection of your whole approach to being at the market. A well thought-out, organized stall will show customers they can trust you *and* your products. In addition you can never go wrong with large, easy to read banners and other signage.

Make sure you also look ready for business. Nothing welcomes customers more than being greeted by a vendor's happy smiling face. Stand up, smile, say good morning, and show them the pride you take in your products, your stall and yourself.

Applying to a Market

$\mathcal{A}$pplying to markets is not particularly difficult, but there are some basic procedures and tactics to use that will give you the best possible chance of getting in. As markets continue to increase in popularity, there will be more competition for spots.

Markets are run two ways. One way is by an autonomous market society that has its own constitution, board of directors, paid memberships and voting privileges. Most market societies are structured as non-profits meaning that all of the money collected must be accounted for, and hopefully used up by the end of each season on things like advertising, infrastructure, market manager's wages, music and special events. Some markets do retain a certain amount of money through to the next year, especially if they have to pay in advance for space rental, insurance and other fees.

The other way is a market run by the local merchants' association. The merchants decide who to invite and what to do with the money from vendors' fees. There are no memberships, no votes, and no board of directors made up of vendors. The merchants handle all of the marketing, the volunteers, space allotment and anything else associated with running the markets.

Both structures can create incredibly successful markets. However, it is good to know whether or not your opinions or complaints will be heard before you voice any opinions on policy or rules. With market societies, you have the right to state your concerns and have changes voted upon during official meetings. For merchant-run markets, any legitimate concerns you have should be considered by conscientious organizers, but there is little recourse if their decisions are not to your liking.

APPLICATION PROCEDURE

Here are the basic steps to follow when applying to markets.

Pick the markets you want to attend.

Fill out the application completely and send it back before the deadline. Sometimes you have to send in your payment with your application.

Go to an adjudication meeting and present your product line.

Wait for confirmation of your acceptance.

Keep a file marked *Market Applications* with the year written on it. For every market you apply to, keep a duplicate copy of the application, and attach all of the rules and regulation to it and keep it in your file. Do the following and keep all these items at the ready for each market you apply for.

1. Make multiple copies of any Food Safe Certificate, yearly health board approval forms, insurance forms, and any supplementary materials required by individual markets.

2. Write up a brief vendor's bio or statement, with an explanation of your products, farm or processing that is unique to your operation.

3. Take photos of you making your products or working in the fields.

4. If possible, ask for letters from rented production facilities stating that you do, indeed, make your products there.

5. Keep copies of any lab reports you have as many markets require these as proof that your value added food products are safe.

6. Make copies of any checks you send for payment and attach them to the application forms

MARKET CHARACTERISTICS

Many markets belong to larger market associations, which may have their own websites listing individual market contact information. You may be familiar with your local markets, but you might need more information for markets an hour or two away from home.

Phone or e-mail the various markets you are considering and ask the market coordinators the following questions:

- How many vendors come to the market each week? How many customers come to a typical market? *Do you want to sell at a market with few customers, or one that is really busy?*

- What is the ratio of locals to tourists? *Are your products meant for locals or for tourists looking for souvenirs? If you are selling pumpkins at a tourist market, how many do you think you'll sell?*

- What is the ratio of stalls for fresh food or farm produce to craft vendors? Does that change throughout the year? Do they have quotas on the numbers of certain kinds of vendors?

- This is a matter of competition and saturation. If you are one of twelve jewelry vendors at a small market, the competition may be fierce. If you are one of only a few vendors, you'll likely be very busy. There seems to be an ideal ratio of the number of vendors to customers. Too many vendors and not enough customers and you'll all be competing for the very few dollars circulating around the market. Too many customers and only a few vendors and the customers get frustrated by not being able to get close to the stalls or the vendors sell out quickly. There is a "sweet spot" that is the magical amount but I'm not sure what that is exactly. You kind of know it when you feel it, and doubly so when the ratio is off.

- Does the market allow for resale or import vendors, and if so what percentage of resale or imports do they allow? Resale is when a vendor buys products at wholesale and resells them to the public. Most markets do not allow this, but some do, so you have to check!

- If markets allow for resale items and imports, it may be very difficult to compete with their prices, so find out who these vendors are, what they sell and if they will likely be in competition with your products.

These questions will give you a good idea of whether or not you'd like to try a particular market. If the person you contact cannot answer any of these questions, it is likely the market board pays little attention to their own market and I would be hesitant to apply if they simply have no information for you.

THE APPLICATION

Most markets operate between March/April to September/October, depending on climate and harvest season. Markets in the southern part of North America may have longer seasons than those up north. Most shut down over the winter. Applications start late in February or early March so you have to be prepared to pay basic application fees and possibly even pay for an entire season's market fees all at one time. Some markets allow for payments to be split up during the season as they sometimes offer seasonal packages. Set aside money early in the spring to pay for your market fees.

When you apply to any market, think of it like a job application. The more prepared and professional you are, the more the people who are adjudicating you will believe that you will follow the rules and behave professionally. Dress neatly and show up on time. Make sure that every piece of information you've been asked to submit is provided in your application. This is crucial! If you do not understand something in the application, phone and ask for clarification before you mail it in. Applications are often rejected based solely on missing information.

If you have special requirements, make sure you have clearly indicated your needs on your application. Some applications provide a place for special requirements, but some do not. Special requirements might include your need for shade because you sell chocolate, or power requirements for your fridge or portable freezer. It might be that you need help because of physical limitations, or need to be away from certain types of vendors due to allergies. Whatever it is, make sure you address your needs in the application, not after you've been accepted and show up to your first market. Also, most markets do not allow you to bring your pets with you, and most have rules about not allowing children to sell products.

ADJUDICATION

Adjudication is when market board members and sometimes non-board volunteers review applications and then invite new vendors to a meeting. Bring a copy of your application, your checkbook, your best work, your sales materials such as flyers and photos of your displays or of you actually making your products, your artist's biography or photos of your farm. You may be given only a five or ten minute interview and may be asked to describe your production process. After you leave, the committee will make their decision and then inform you whether or not you've been accepted.

Remember that if you do not get in, it may only be because of the overall mix of vendors that the market organizers want and may have nothing to do with your products. It might be that your products are not as well developed or refined as they could be or the adjudicators may not be qualified to truly judge your products' artistic merits. Many adjudicators are also vendors, some of who may be selling products similar to yours. Committee run adjudications prevent conflict of interest issues.

Whatever the reason for any rejection of your application, try to keep an open mind and ask for an explanation as to why you did not get in. You may want to apply to several markets if you are uncertain of your products' acceptability. Once you've been approved at a market one year, you will likely get in again the next year even though you have to reapply from year to year. You will usually have to get approval only for any new products you want to sell. Most markets do not allow vendors to add products at will without getting prior approval. This is to prevent unfair competition after the board has chosen its mix of vendors. If someone sells plants and then suddenly decides to bring their knitted socks to sell, they might be infringing upon another vendor whose main product is hand-knitted garments.

Once you have been accepted as a vendor at a market, however, you need to remember the following points:

- A signed market application is a contract. It is your *agreement* to follow the rules of that market. Follow the rules or do not come. If you do not like the rules, then become a member of the market society, voice your concerns at official meetings, and then vote for change.

- No matter how many years you've done a market, you do not *own* a particular space unless you have a signed contract stating otherwise. Accept that you may be moved from time to time. If a particular space is that important to you, be sure to mention it in the special requirements section on your application. Customers will find you if they really want to.

- Do not complain about market policies to the public. Discuss it with board members in private and always put your concerns in writing. If someone has a serious concern about you or your products, then do not respond to their concerns until you have something in writing from *them*. This is so important: GET IT IN WRITING!

- If you have general problems with another vendor, try to settle your own affairs. Only if that fails should you ask the market manager to mediate.

TYPES OF VENDORS

If you are not comfortable signing up for a full season package, a good option is to be a drop-in vendor. You have to apply to the market the same way as fulltime vendors, but mark down that you want to be a drop-in vendor instead of a package holder or full-time vendor.

DROP-IN VENDORS

Most markets allocate a few extra spaces for drop-ins and can also place them in fulltime vendors' spots when they are absent from the market on a given week. Drop-in spots are assigned in two ways. It is either first come first served, or assigned, depending on what you sell. Most markets give priority to fresh food vendors before value-added food or craft vendors. Some markets allow you to sign up for individual dates during the season but you have to know which dates you want in advance. That's hard if you're not sure what produce you'll have in any given week or if you've got other commitments.

To get a drop-in spot, you call the market coordinator or manager on the specified call-in day and ask for a spot. You will be put on the list and then informed if you get a spot. If the market is held on a Saturday, the call-in day is usually no later than Thursday. Do not wait too late in the day to call for a drop-in spot because they'll likely all be taken first thing in the morning.

Drop-ins pay for their stall on the day they come, and costs are usually higher than if you'd bought a package. The manager will come around to collect payment and you may need to pay this first thing in the morning so be sure to have a checkbook or enough cash and ask for a receipt. Drop-ins are also an option for vendors who may not have enough cash flow to pay up front for a full package deal or if vendors are not sure whether the market will be good for them. It is an excellent way to start, but you have to stay on top of call-in days and get your name in as soon as they let you start calling in for a spot.

Expect to be in a different spot every week if you are a drop-in. Customers may have a hard time finding you from week to week, so make sure your tent is easily recognizable. One method is to put up a tall flag onto your stall. People can see it from a distance and you can remind people to look for the flag when they come back the next week. When I did drop-ins, I always set up and then walked around the market letting fellow vendors know where I was set up so they could direct people to me if customers asked where I was. This worked out well for me and friendly vendors are usually helpful. If you do not do this though, some of the fulltime vendors might not know you are there if they do not see you from their stalls.

One of the best things about being a drop-in vendor is that if you do not want to go one week, you simply do not call in. You can do different markets each week, and you get new neighbors all the time. I enjoyed moving around, being in different parts of the market. It made the market new each time and allowed for greater flexibility than if I'd simply bought a package and stayed in one place all the time. The worst thing to do, though, is to call in for a space and then bail out at the last minute. You may not be allowed in again unless you had a legitimate excuse that you can back up with proof.

PACKAGE DEALS

Packages are usually cheaper on a day-to-day basis than drop-ins and you often get the same spot each week. This creates consistency for your customers and for you. You simply show up on market day, unload, park and set up. If you cannot attend one week, you have to call or e-mail as far in advance as you can so the market coordinator can offer your spot to a drop-in vendor. Otherwise you are required to show up, rain or shine. If you bail out on a market day, you may be given a written warning and may even be suspended if you do it again. If you are sick or have a family emergency, phone the market as soon as you know. This kind of thing does happen, and most markets will not penalize you for legitimate absences.

CONCLUSION

Applying to markets is generally straightforward, and with a little planning you can develop a system for applying that will be consistent from market to market. Experiment by attending a few different markets in your area as a drop-in vendor if you are not sure about committing to a full time package deal. You will quickly see which ones work best for you. Then you can decide which markets to do the following year.

Hilary Huntley, of Trial By Fire pottery, with her freshly made mugs

Hand made wooden bowls make a unique product

Attending Your First Market

$\mathscr{I}$f you have never done a market before, there are some steps to run through so you'll know what to expect on your first day. This chapter will help you get organized from the night before the market until you are back home after your first day.

Remember, you are not the only one trying to load and unload. Not everyone is fast or efficient and there may be many vendors who act like the market rules do not apply to them.

Have patience. Help out anyone you see who is really struggling and remember to be polite. There may come a day when you need someone else's help and you'll be more likely to receive it if you are patient, courteous and professional.

PREPARING THE NIGHT BEFORE

Careful preparation the night before a market will make market day smooth and trouble free.

1. Load your vehicle the night before if you are parked in a secure area and your items will not be in danger of freezing or getting wet. Some people load their basic stall supplies, but leave the stock until the morning. If there is a good chance of rain, make sure the *last* thing you pack is a

big tarp so you can take it out first and lay it down so you can put your products on top. Then you can cover them up so they do not get wet.

2. Make sure you have enough fuel in your vehicle and check the tire pressure if you will have a heavy load. Do *not* wait till morning to get gas, especially on your first day. I guarantee you will simply not have enough time.

3. Make a lunch, get water and a thermos ready and set your coffee maker. Set out your warm clothing, waterproof boots, hats, gloves, and parka. *Always* take a warm, windproof jacket, unless you know it will be a scorching hot day. Even a beautiful morning can frequently turn cold, windy and stormy by midmorning or afternoon. I simply cannot stress this enough: take warm clothes with you, even if you do not use them. You'll be so happy you did if the weather becomes inclement.

4. Put your float (cash) box into the bag you are taking to the market and put it by the front door so you do not forget it. Make sure to get enough float prior to the market. I always replenish my float when I do my bank deposits after the previous week's market.

5. Review how to get to the market if you have never been there before and set a time by which you'll have to leave in order to arrive well within the time allotted to you for loading in. Just don't be late to market or you might have to load in by hand if you can't bring your vehicle onsite.

6. Go to bed early and get a good night's rest.

AT THE MARKET

Prepare to spend the entire day at the market.

1. Get up, shower, shave if you have to, and dress neatly. Eat a good, hearty breakfast. You'll need it!

2. Finish loading your vehicle. Remember to take your samples, your lunch, thermos, water and your float box. Put in your tarp last if it is raining.

3. Drive to the market, check in, and ask where your spot is. Drive in, unload your stuff, but keep your float box with you in the car out of sight. Once you've unloaded, go park your car if you have to park offsite. Then walk back and set up when you are allowed to. There is usually a cut off time when all cars have to be off the market site so be sure to focus on efficiently unloading your car.

4. Set up your tent before you set up any tables, etc. If you set up your tables first, it is much harder to navigate your tent around and over your stuff without knocking things over.

5. Secure the tent from the wind with weights or tie downs, and put up your side walls if you want. Some markets allow you to set up your tent early if it is raining so your items do not get damaged.

6. Set up your tables, cover with tablecloths, risers and any major structural systems first. Put up your banner.

7. Set out your products and signs.

8. Prepare any sampling you are doing and then survey the results. Take pictures of your stall and review them a few times to get a set up that works best. Experiment with your set up and move items around until you create a look and flow that works best for you.

9. Place your personal items securely away and, if you need to, go to the bathroom, get a refill on your coffee, take a quick walk through the market to see who is there and then get back to your stall. Some produce vendors take a walk around to compare weekly pricing and then go back to their stalls and set their produce prices for the day. Your market may have pricing policies so that no one vendor will severely undercut or overprice their produce. Check the market rules or ask someone what is typical at this market.

10. Sell your products and stay focused on business.

11. Ensure you are well hydrated, eat your lunch, and add electrolytes to your water if it is a particularly hot day. Emergen-C is a company that sells individual packages of Vitamin C and electrolytes that you can

easily tuck into your lunch or keep in your First Aid kit. Gatorade type products are another option, but I find them too high in sugar. The electrolytes will help you retain essential body salts lost through sweating.

12. Wait until the official end of market day before you start breaking down your stall, even if it is a slow day. If you start packing up early, you may be given a warning. It is okay to slowly start "tidying" up by breaking down empty boxes, and organizing, but keep products available for sale. Markets are very strict about this. Stay open for business right till the end of the day.

13. Once the market is done for the day, do everything in reverse. Clean up sampling stations. Take down signs, pack remaining product, dismantle tables and display and take down tent.

SAFETY NOTE: keep a close eye on your personal belongings and on your float box. Keep them in a covered box out of sight. Once your entire stall is broken down, including your tent, take your personal belongings, get your car, and then line up to load out.

14. It may take a while before those ahead of you manage to get their stuff loaded up. If someone in front of you is particularly slow and blocking traffic, go help him or her. The market manager should be directing traffic!

15. Once you get to your stall, put your personal items into the front of your car out of sight or even lock the door. Load up the vehicle as fast as you can, check the area to make sure you did not leave anything behind, and if necessary, sweep the space if you dropped a lot of refuse on the ground.

16. Drive home.

AFTER THE MARKET

1. If you are only doing one market a week, unload as soon as you get home because I guarantee that you'll not want to do it once you put your feet up.

2. Dispose of left over samples, clean sampling dishes and put them right back into the demo box. Replenish any needed supplies right away so you are not missing supplies the next time you are at the market.

3. Take out all the money from your float box, count out the float and return it to the box. Count the remaining money and record your revenue in a market revenue book. Some people record every sale they make including the price and compare their final tally with their sales record. The figures should match. If you borrowed money from your float, repay it from personal money, not market revenue. Calculate any taxes you have collected and place the taxes into a separate envelope to send to the government. Put the rest of the market revenue into a bank deposit envelope for deposit the following week. Set out any large bills in your float so that you can get smaller bills and coin at the bank when you are making your deposit.

4. Review what sold best, what did not sell, and make plans for next week's market.

Congratulations! You just completed your first day at the market!

Many vendors do three to five markets a week and may not unload their vehicles at the end of the day. That will depend much on where you live, how safe it is to leave items in your car overnight or if the weather cooperates. You will find this system easier as you go along, but it helps to have a plan so you minimize the risks of forgetting necessary supplies.

MAKING YOUR MARKET DAY EASIER

- If it is raining, the *last* thing to pack into your truck is a big tarp. When you are unloading at the market put it on the ground, set down your stock and fold the tarp over top to keep the rain off. Better yet, keep all your stock and supplies in covered plastic bins.

- When unloading, organize your gear in the *opposite* way you are going to set up. If you put your tables down first and *then* stack all your stock on top of them, you'll first have to move all your stuff *off* the tables in order to set up the tables. Unload your tables, risers and shelves so you do not have to move other things out of the way to set them up. This will save you a lot of time moving stuff around. It is almost a guarantee that if you have anyone "helping" you, they will inevitably put things where you do not want them. Save your nerves and send them to park the car and get you a coffee.

- Be conscious of using good posture. Lift with your legs, do not twist and lift at the same time, and if items are just too heavy, divide them into smaller containers that you can manage. Use both hands to carry heavy objects. Be especially careful not to drop things on your toes.

Keep a pair of nail clippers in your cash box. [Yup, I break nails all the time loading and unloading stuff.]

- Be aware of the natural flow of market energies. Mornings are very busy for fresh food vendors, but may not pick up until late morning for crafters or value-added food vendors. Be prepared for a slow start to the day if you are not selling fresh food. It also does not seem to matter if the market ends at 2:00 or 3:00 or 4:00 pm because the last hour tends to be quiet.

- Every market day is different. Sometimes there is a happy, lively vibrancy where customers are enthusiastic and in the mood for spending money. On other days, people walk around staring into space. Try not to judge one market harshly based on only one day. Give a market a chance. Early spring may be slow, but come July, the market atmosphere could be very busy and exciting. After one season you should be aware of the rhythms that change and flow from one market to another, from one day to the next, and from hour to hour.

- Be careful of how much money you spend on market treats. If you are watching your money, buying coffee, buns, lunch and snacks quickly adds up. Bringing your own coffee, lunch and treats will save you a lot of money and may be healthier than eating cinnamon buns and grilled sausages each week.

- Finally, always keep market revenue separate from personal money. If you "borrow" money from your float, leave an IOU and replace it later from personal funds.

ESSENTIALS TO TAKE WITH YOU

Here is a list of some essential items to take with you to the market.

- Anti-fatigue mats. Get a set at a local hardware store. They'll save your back and legs and insulate your feet from extremely hot or cold ground.

- Place all necessary paperwork in plastic sheet protectors and put them in a binder. Include copies of your health forms, food safe certificate, lab results, permits or any other document that you may be required to show.

- You may have to display health forms and permits. Laminate them, punch holes in the top, string them together with binder rings, and hang them from one of the tent struts.

- Always take your tent's sidewalls with you. You never know if it is going to rain, or the sun will be too hot on your backside. They are also handy if you want to block off a vendor you would prefer to avoid.

- The wind can cause havoc. Take heavy weights to weigh down your tent. Tents are notorious for flipping over in the wind and can damage other vendor's wares. I use 8" square concrete landscaping blocks with a hole in the middle. I put one at each corner, put the tent leg inside it and put the block on top of the tent foot. Alternatively, fill gallon milk jugs with water or sand and set them on top of the tent feet. Sometimes even this is not enough. Some vendors hold their tents down with extra rope attached to dumbbells or downrigger weights. Others bungee their tent legs to another vendor's tent or to a railing, poles or anything they can attach to their tent. Be prepared.

- Take a selection of bungee cords to attach banners, to hold down the tent or to attach your neighbors' tent to yours on really windy days.

- Bring a tall folding bar stool so you can sit, but remain relatively upright when customers walk by. You can get them at IKEA.

- Bring pens, note book, receipt book, calculator, laminated pricing signs, flyers or business cards, a small First Aid kit with bee sting remedy, facial tissue, nail clippers, feminine hygiene supplies, electrolyte pouches, sunscreen and any medications you may need during the day.

- All vendors are required to take out any garbage they create during the day so bring a small garbage can and bags. I used to put a garbage bin in front of my stall, but customers ended up putting in everything from full cups of coffee to left over ice cream and sandwiches. This attracted the wasps. The day I took home a dirty diaper was the day I stopped putting out a large garbage container.

- Use small containers and empty them out as needed into a larger container behind your table. The market should provide customers with adequate garbage containers so mention it to them if there are not enough available.

- Bring a foldable dolly (or hand truck) if your stall is far from where you park your car.

- If you are a food vendor and give out samples of your wares, set up a basic hand washing station and use it frequently. Your local health board should provide you with guidelines, but here is what works well for me:

  ◊ A small, sturdy folding table.

  ◊ Large camping water container with a free flowing spigot.

  ◊ Liquid pump soap, preferable with little to no scent. The top twists closed so it can't ooze soap out into my demo box at the end of the day.

◊   Single use paper towel on a stand so it does not fall over.

◊   A tall bucket to catch the used water.

◊   Hand sanitizer.

◊   Spray bottle with a mild bleach solution for sanitizing any dropped utensils and spraying off your concrete blocks if a dog pees on them. That stops other dogs from peeing on them as well.

◊   Unscented hand lotion that sinks into the skin quickly and does not leave a greasy film on your hands.

◊   A box of disposable, vinyl gloves if you are handling food directly.

A hand washing station is of no use unless you actually use it. Wash your hands frequently. At the end of the day, you can usually dump the water down a sewer drain or on some plants if you've used a biodegradable soap, but if the market does not allow this, put the lid on the water, take it home and dump it down the drain. Catering carts usually have more stringent requirements so this system is only relevant for basic sampling.

FOOD VENDORS

Handing out samples to the public is one of the best ways to sell a food product. It is important, though, to plan your sampling strategy carefully.

The point of sampling is *not* to fill the customer up. If you give them too large a sample, they might be satisfied enough that they do not even want the item any more. You want to entice customers with just enough of your product that they simply have to buy something.

A tiny sample is enough. When I sample my mustards, all I do is dip a toothpick into the jar and hand the toothpick to the customer. Really, how much more do they need? They either like it or they do not.

Remember sampling is a business expense and you want it to be as efficient and cost effective as possible. You need to carefully control your samples and be aware of food safety issues.

FOOD SAFETY

Depending on where you live, your public health inspector may or may not be highly involved in regulating and policing your market. It may be that while the inspector approves your yearly health permits, it will be the market manager's job to regulate and enforce food safety rules. It is up to you to develop and maintain a simple, safe and effective method for giving samples of your product.

While you can make sure your own hands are clean, there is no way to know how clean your customers' are. It takes only one person with Hepatitis to infect hundreds. This can happen quite easily if your samples are set out in a communal dish where people's bare hands can touch numerous samples leaving bacteria, viruses, fecal matter, bodily fluids or any other contaminants behind for the next person to ingest.

The public is unaware of the risks of communal sampling so it is up to you to take the steps to keep everyone safe. Unfortunately, I have often seen vendors who are less than scrupulous about keeping their hands clean so please develop a system for constantly tracking your cleanliness.

CONTROLLING THE SAMPLES

Here are the most important points to remember when offering samples:

- Never let *anyone* touch any of your samples with bare hands (including yourself).

- Keep all samples separated in individual pill cups or keep them well separated on a tray and skewered with a single use toothpick. Use tongs to distribute samples onto a tray.

- Skewer individual samples with toothpicks and hand them out piece by piece instead of leaving them on a tray. This way you control both the sampling and the number of pieces each customer eats. If you set out a plate of samples, customers frequently eat multiple samples when all they really needed is one.

- Never turn a toothpick over and use the opposite end for another sample because it has already been touched. Dollar stores often have boxes of 1000 toothpicks, so stock up and use a new toothpick for each sample.

- Use a sneeze shield to protect your samples and prevent customers from sticking their fingers into them. A sneeze shield is a clear plastic or glass barrier set between you and your customers to prevent customers from sneezing on or touching your products. Bakers and anyone selling foods open to the air use them.

- Have your sneeze shield made to your specifications by a local plastics shop or buy a clear acrylic display box that you can place on its side and use as a barrier between you and your customers.

- Use a gloved hand to lay out tiny plastic tasting spoons, and set them out so that customers only touch the handle. Do not just dump them into a basket.

- Know that even if you put out a basket full of crackers and a set of tongs for customers to use, they will not use the tongs. They'll simply just pick up a cracker with their fingers.

- Make sure to have a small, visible garbage container for the public to drop their toothpicks, tasting cups and spoons.

- People have allergies and food sensitivities and yet, given a free, easily accessible sample, customers may sample your products without having checked for potential allergens. This is especially true of children.

- Display a prominent sign indicating any potential allergens and request that all customers inform you of any allergies prior to sampling. In fact, I always tell customers when a specific product contains nuts *prior* to releasing the sample into their hands.

- NEVER give children samples without permission from the adult with them. If a child asks for a sample, tell them to go get their adult and bring them back. This is for two reasons, the first of which is food safety. The second is that the adult is the one with the money.

- Avoid mixing dry dips with sour cream or yogurt because they'll quickly go bad in warm weather. Most markets do not allow dairy based dips to be served as samples unless there is mechanical refrigeration in your stall and you do not have the samples out for more than about ten minutes at a time.

- Hard plastic sampling trays are better than disposable paper or plastic because they can be cleaned and reused.

- Have at least two sets of tongs, metal spoons or trays in your demo kit in case they get dirty. Keep the clean ones in a clean re-sealable bag with CLEAN written on it. At the end of the day, put the dirty ones into the second bag with DIRTY written on it. When you get home, take the dirty dishes and utensils out of the bag, wash them carefully and then put them back into the clean bag so they are ready to go for the next market day.

CONCLUSION

A day selling at a market can be fun, profitable and exhausting. Be realistic and prepare well beforehand so that your market day is as good as it can be. It is normal to forget items once in a while, but if you forget something every market day, do not be surprised if other vendors start looking the other way when you once again ask for coins or small bills for your float or other supplies you always seem to forget.

Sampling is one of the very best ways of selling product, but be smart about it and do not give away the store. Sample only enough to let people get an idea of what you are selling. All they need is a small bite, a taste of what is possible and then they will be hooked.

Controlled, thoughtful sampling, coupled with an effective sales pitch can sell the product.

Hand made paper maché

Handling Difficult Situations

$\mathscr{M}$ost days the market is a wonderful environment, but unexpected things do happen. This chapter will prepare you for some issues you may face and suggest how to deal with them.

People sometimes trip, fall and get injured. Tents sometimes flip over in the wind and damage vendors' wares. Homeless people ask for money, and shoplifters or pickpockets sometimes work the markets. You might have to deal with complaints, rudeness and tricky conflicts with other vendors. Sometimes you even have to deal with the emotions of having a bad sales day and find professional ways of coping so that you do not affect other vendors.

COPING WITH THE UNEXPECTED

Dealing with these issues can require considerable tact and self-control, so here are some tips for getting through potentially difficult situations.

ACCIDENTS

- Accidents sometimes occur. Customers cut themselves on something, slip and fall, hit their heads, trip over displays or even have allergic reactions to your products.

  ◊ Make sure your liability insurance is in place. Market insurance usually only covers when someone falls or gets hurt at the market, but not for what is called "product liability." If someone gets injured or sick as a result of using your products, you need to have your own insurance in case of any legal action taken against you. Check with your insurance broker on the potential risks your products may pose and invest in the appropriate insurance policy.

  ◊ Update your basic First Aid Certificate or find out who the designated First Aid attendant is at the market. If there isn't one, then insist that someone on the board acts as one or volunteer to be a First Aid attendant yourself. Keep a basic First Aid kit at your stall at all times and include ointment for insect stings.

  ◊ If you need to administer First Aid, get the market manager to come right away. Ask if another vendor saw the accident and ask them to write down what they remember in case someone needs to make a statement to the authorities. If it is really serious, call the paramedics right away.

  ◊ Ask permission before you touch someone to administer First Aid unless they are unconscious. If they are with someone else, ask *that* person if it is okay to help them.

  ◊ If you are shaken or upset about the incident, tell another vendor right away and then take some time to sit down and relax. Sometimes you can go into shock from simply observing an accident so let someone know if you are feeling shaky, sweaty or faint.

- Tents and displays can fly all over the place in the wind. Always secure your tent legs with weights, tie tents together, or attach tents to poles, railings or whatever else you can attach them to. I see it happen at least once every year where someone's tent or displays flip right over, crashing into and breaking other vendors' stuff.

- You are responsible for setting up your stall safely so get someone to help you if the weather is not cooperating! If your tent flips over and breaks someone else's stock, you might be liable for the damages your tent or display causes. Find out if the market's insurance or your own liability insurance covers this.

THEFT

- Sometimes people shoplift, or they work in teams whereby one distracts you and another person steals something when you are not looking their way.

- If you witness someone stealing from your stall, call the police and keep the shoplifter in sight until police arrive. You have the right to protect your property, but you just never know what a thief will do. They may have a weapon or injure you in some way so let the police do their job. If you can, alert other vendors or the market manager to keep an eye on the person until the police arrive.

- Some market managers photograph shoplifters who come back more than once, so review any photos of proven shoplifters and keep a watchful eye.

- Keep your most expensive items attached securely to display boards. Place marbles inside glassware or pottery so they rattle when picked up. Keep valuable goods in a locked cabinet, showing them one at a time. If you have a really busy stall, consider having a second person there to help.

- If you did not see someone take anything, but are certain that the item is missing after a particular customer leaves, inform your market manager. Point out the individual and have them watched carefully to see if they continue wandering the market for more opportunities. Inform other vendors that an alleged thief is in the market, but be discreet because you could be wrong!

- Shoplifters generally do not like it when you pay too much attention to them. If you get a bad vibe from someone, make sure you look them straight in the eye to let them know that you see them. They often do not like this and will move on to someone who is not paying close attention to their wares.

- Be vigilant about safeguarding your personal belongings and float box. Keep purses and wallets in covered bins. Remove large bills from your float box and keep them in a secure place preferably in a zippered pocket on your body. Dividing up the money means that if your float box is stolen, you will not lose everything all at once.

- If you have to leave your stall unattended, close and lock your float box, put it away and inform one of your neighbors that you'll be gone for a few minutes.

- Never display your float box in the open, even if you are with other people. Thieves scope places out to see who works alone and may prey on vendors who are oblivious of their surroundings.

- Vehicles do get broken into frequently, so never leave money, float boxes or any personal documents, wallets, etc. in your car.

DONATIONS

- Sometimes people beg for money or food. Feel free to say: *"Sorry, no."* While charity is admirable, you are not working alone at the market. There are other vendors who may not appreciate your charity if it ends up bringing more people looking for handouts.

- If begging is an issue in your community, consider forming a market charity box accessible once the market is over for the day. Alternatively, contact a local food bank or charity organization and let them know that your market has organized a weekly donation box that they can collect and then let the person wanting charity know they can access free items through that association.

- People often ask for donations of either money or product for a great cause. They always say: *"It'll be great exposure for your company!"* Maybe yes, and maybe no. It is nice to give, but once you have been known to give away product or money, expect to see more people heading your way. I get dozens of requests for donations a year. It can get expensive to do this. Analyze how beneficial a donation will be to your company.

    ◊ What is really in it for *you*? Do you have donations built into your business finances? If you are not in the business of giving away free product or money choose your donations wisely and really decide if it is worth it. What kind of *exposure*, exactly, will you get? Print media, television, radio, widely distributed flyers or a mere mention during a high school reunion dance when no one can hear the announcer because the music's so loud?

◊ Will your donation attract the attention of potential wholesale accounts? Will it help spread the word about your products to those who would most likely *buy* your products?

◊ A gracious way of saying *'no'* is to say: *"I appreciate you thinking of me but my donation allocation is full for the year. Good luck with the event."*

◊ Do not feel guilty for not giving out donations if you do not want to. It is *your* business and you have to be able to afford it and feel comfortable with it. All you need to say is: *"Thanks for thinking of me, but no thank you. Good luck with your event."* If you find this is becoming a problem at the market, inform your market manager and ask them to deal with the individuals scoping the market for donations.

VENDOR CONFLICT

• It is *never* a neighboring vendor's fault if you lose something while you are away from your stall, even if you asked them to watch while you go to the bathroom. If you ask someone to watch your stall, get back as fast as you can. You can develop trusting relationships with many vendors and for the most part, people will keep watch if they are not busy. Just do not burden busy vendors with this request. They simply will not have the time to watch.

• Similarly, if you are uncomfortable watching someone else's stuff, let them know you'll not be responsible if they lose something. If they ask you to watch their booth, make sure you find out if they've put away their money and say, "*I'll do my best but I can't guarantee that I'll be able to watch your booth.*"

- Sometimes arguments happen between vendors. The reasons are many, but usually have to do with space allotment, or blocking stall space when a vendor puts their display too far out in front of another vendor's stall. Vendors can also be an impatient lot when dealing with those who pack up slowly at the end of the day or block traffic with their vehicles.

  ◊ Deal with it badly and you may actually jeopardize your *own* status at the market. Petty feuds between vendors can last for years, creating tension and bad energy, so it is worthwhile to learn how to deal with issues tactfully.

  ◊ The most important thing to remember is that every vendor is running their own little store even if you are side by side. It pays to be courteous, firm and avoid petty bickering that will only serve to make *you* look bad.

  ◊ Do not complain about vendors in front of other vendors or in front of the public. People form friendships at the market and it *will* get back to them.

  ◊ Deal with issues that arise directly with the person in question. So often I hear vendors complaining about another vendor. However, when asked, I discover that they've never even *spoken* to that person directly about the problem! Never approach a market manager about an issue with another vendor until you've tried to work it out on your own first. Of course, if you feel truly threatened by someone, do not take any risks; call the market manager. That is so rare though and most conflicts can be resolved on your own.

  ◊ Do not get involved in a conflict between other vendors unless it directly involves you. Mind your own business and if someone tries to drag you into it, ask if they've tried to work it out on their own. If they say 'yes' and it cannot be solved, then direct them to the market manager. Whatever happens, stay out of it!

◊ Sometimes you simply do not like another vendor, even if they've done nothing wrong or have not broken any rules. All you can do is put up your sidewalls and try your best to ignore them.

◊ If a vendor has a personal habit that is directly affecting your sales, then you should say something. For example, if you are finding it hard to hear your customers because a neighboring vendor is talking really loudly and howling with laughter all day, try saying something like, *"I appreciate that you are having a great time in your stall, but could you please keep the volume down just a little. I am having a hard time hearing my customers."*

◊ Most vendors' behavior is unconscious and they likely have no idea that they are impeding your ability to make sales. If that is the case, find a polite way of addressing this. On the other hand, ask yourself if you are just being irritable and overly picky. We all have a few irritating habits. Try to regulate your behavior and think about how you are affecting others around you.

◊ Apologize if you lose your temper. Never say, *"I'm sorry, but . . ."* You need to *mean* it, because an empty apology just makes things worse. No one deserves to be on the receiving end of someone else's outburst and it has no place in a professional environment.

◊ Finally, cultivate some patience. Offer help to those who need it, take a deep breath, and think twice before you say some choice words you may regret later. The day may come when your own tent flips and you need the help of the same person you chewed out the week before.

CUSTOMER COMPLAINTS

- Customers do complain from time to time, bring back product or broken or defective merchandise, or they simply did not like what they bought and want to return it.

  ◊ Many people who buy produce from regular supermarkets are buying produce that was never ripe to begin with and may be treated with chemicals to make them last longer. They may be use to produce lasting for weeks in the fridge with nary a black spot. If you sell items that must be eaten within a day, make sure to inform customers that the products will go bad unless they eat them right away.

  ◊ If this is a recurring problem for you, post a clearly visible sign in your stall saying something like: *"Our products are picked at the peak of freshness. Use products within 24 hours of purchase."* This will inform customers of the relative delicacy of your products *prior* to purchase and will avoid the possibility of customers coming back later to say that they were not told that their raspberries would go moldy three days after purchase.

  ◊ If something you've made breaks, fix it or give them a replacement. Do the repairs right away, call them when it is done and remember to bring it back to the market for them the next week. If they live far away, ask them to mail it to you, fix it, and then mail it back with a refund on their postage or even a refund on the whole item if it caused them considerable problems. Make a commitment to provide them with better service than they'd ever get from a large, impersonal corporation.

  ◊ Be sure that delicate items are well wrapped and tell the customer to be especially careful with them. Provide written care tips attached to the receipt, give a copy to the customer and keep one for yourself. If they come back with a dead plant, and no receipt, you are covered. Clearly post your transaction rules in your stall and on sales receipts and make sure your customers are aware of these rules *prior* to purchase. No refunds, no plant guarantees, no exchange without receipt, final sale, cash only, are all acceptable transaction rules, but only if they are posted and written on the receipt!

◊　If you create personalized or custom made orders, make sure to get a deposit that at *least* covers the cost of the product. Many vendors require a 50% deposit or even more. Make sure that the order form clearly states that the item is non-refundable or if they cancel the order, the deposit is non-refundable. You must have their written signature and all the conditions must be *in writing* to be sure they cannot come back later and accuse you of deceptive marketing.

◊　Buy a sales order book with triplicate copies, write up the order, take and mark the payment for the deposit, get their signature, phone number, address, and give them the top copy so that every base is covered. While I'm not a legal expert, it makes sense to write things down and give copies to everyone involved so there is no confusion later on.

◊　Some customers refuse to pay taxes. A fellow vendor told me that one customer got so angry that she was charging sales taxes, he accused her of pocketing the tax money. He slammed down only enough money for the cost of the item and took off with the product. That is called theft. She is a sensitive woman not used to this kind of conflict so she just let the guy go. Call the police if this *ever* happens to you!

◊　The only solution to this kind of resistance is to build the tax directly into the cost of the product and clearly post this fact in your stall with a sign that says: *"Prices include tax."* That way the customer has no choice but to pay the entire cost and will likely not argue the point.

•　It is easy to receive accolades and congratulations on great product, but one rarely grows or improves from these experiences. Instead, welcome complaints as an opportunity to show superior customer service and bend over backwards to make your customers happy. Sometimes, it is true, it is the customer's fault, but they will be the one who has to live with being dishonest. If someone complains, try to refund money, offer free product, pay for shipping or otherwise find a way to go above and beyond their expectations.

You simply cannot pay for the level of goodwill this will foster. Do whatever you can to make it right and more if you can afford it.

- It is also common for organizers of other markets, shows or special events to come and solicit for vendors. It is fine to take their information, but thoroughly check them out before committing to an event you've never heard of. They often ask you to hand out flyers *for* them and it does not take long before your stall gets cluttered with other people's flyers. It is perfectly okay to say: *"Thanks for the interest, I'll take one flyer and keep it for reference, but I do not display other people's flyers, sorry."* Some market organizations also do not allow vendors to display advertising from other markets or shows, so be sure to review your market policies.

DISTRACTIONS

- Customers or friends sometimes hang around your stall too long when what you really want is to get on with sales. How do you get rid of someone politely?

    ◊ If someone is talking up a storm, oblivious to your need to make a living, just say something simple like: *"Sorry to interrupt. It's been great seeing you again, but I really do have to pay attention to attracting some customers. Give me your number and I'll call you later."*

◊ If a person comes every week expecting to eat all your samples, but never buys anything, try this: *"Hello again, I see you come back every week and like my products. You must know your favorite by now so can I wrap that up for you to buy this week?"* It is bold, but still welcoming. It lets them know that *you* remember how many times they've been there already, and that you are actually there to sell, not to give away product.

◊ Another issue is when children ask for samples and then want another one, and another one. Often the adult does not say a word and just lets the child continue demanding samples. A simple way of cutting this short is by saying the following; *"Did you like that first sample I gave you?"* The kid will nod yes, of course. *"Well, then these bags are $10.00 so maybe your mom will buy some for you."* This will snap the parent out of it and quick. They'll either buy something, or move on.

> I am not suggesting that every customer is greedy, but it's true that given free access to samples, some people will eat every single sample and then move to the next table without buying anything. It's up to you to decide whether you're there to make money, or operate a food bank.

◊ Here is another classic. A lot of people have no intention of buying anything at the market; they are there as something to do to pass the time and it is easy to see who they are. They usually have no purse or shopping bags, often have their arms crossed in front of them or hands stuffed into pockets. They also walk slowly, looking around without any purposeful intent and often with an air that says, *"I'm just hangin' around."* They ask for samples, ask a million questions and then start complementing you on how amazing you are to have started your business. After you've spent 15 minutes talking to them, they often say, *"Okay, well thanks, and have a good day,"* and then they leave. In the meantime, you've totally ignored any number of potential, real customers who might have actually wanted to buy something. The simple way to cut short this kind of person is to say, *"So, are you doing lots of shopping today?"* Say it politely and with genuine kindness. It is a polite question and every single time I say this, the people look down at their hands and say, *"Oh, we are just looking today,"* and then walk off. It might sound a little harsh to say this, but I'm not there to chat all day with people who have no intention of buying, but who are quite happy to take up *my* entire day. It is serious business for me and I do need to focus my attention on people who are interested in buying. Still, it pays to be polite since you never really know if someone will eventually come back. It never serves anyone to be rude.

◊ If you are busy chit chatting, text messaging, knitting or otherwise preoccupied, customers will not come into your stall because they think you are too busy to care if they are there or not. The main question is whether you are actually there to sell, or not. Please also consider that the way you behave in your stall affects the entire market around you. Customers will form the impression that vendors are bored or not interested in being there if they see vendor after vendor staring off into space or reading books. So why should they stay? Your attitude at the market affects the entire market and everyone's ability to make sales and create a welcoming environment for customers.

◊ Most neighboring vendors respectfully stop chatting when customers arrive, so be aware of this and get out of the way if you are the one chatting with a neighbor. If an inexperienced vendor does not get this, you'll have to explain it gently: *"No offence, but when customers come I need to pay attention to them. I may just stop talking to you so I can attend to business."* Just be aware of when you might be taking up too much of another vendor's time. If you see them avoiding your gaze or busily rearranging their products whenever you come over, this is a big hint that they really do not want you there.

◊ Sometimes it can be hard not to be drawn into a long conversation, especially if it is a slow day. Be aware, though, that if you are so busy talking, you may miss the chance of attracting customers into your stall; customers do not usually like interrupting vendors who are deeply in conversation, so they'll likely just walk straight by. I often attract customers from 10 feet out front of my stall. I could never do that if I were so distracted by a conversation. Save important conversations for when you are not at market.

    ◊   A final note is to remind you to keep your personal stuff private. We often do share personal issues with other vendors, but if you have lots of problems in your life, please consider that professional counseling might be more appropriate than using the market as weekly therapy.

- Sometimes a customer just seems to want to argue. You have a particular product and they think you should make something else. You are not using organic ingredients so they think it is their mission to lecture you. You have one size and they think you should make another. I've heard it *all*, really. As a captive "audience", some people are quite happy to stand there all day and lecture you, but never have any intention of buying a product. How do you handle these situations?

    ◊   You have to politely interrupt them and tell them: *"Well, thanks for your opinions and suggestion. I also really do need to focus on my business. Thanks for stopping by."* Stop talking and start moving boxes, arranging your display, or pick up your phone and call someone or simply start talking to people walking by.

    ◊   Sometimes people really do have some good suggestions, but you simply do not have the time to devote to a detailed discussion on the matter. Tell them this and if you want to continue the discussion, ask for their phone number and arrange to call them later or ask them to put their ideas into an e-mail and send them to you.

- If they simply want to argue, and do not get your hints, you will just have to be more firm and ask them to leave. It is rare, but it does happen. *"I see you have strong opinions and I appreciate that. I am, also going to have to ask you to move along so I can focus on my job. Thanks."* You have the right to run your business as you see fit, and while it is interesting to be on the receiving end of some unsolicited "advice" or criticism, ultimately you are the one who makes the decisions for your business.

◊ The easiest way of handling argumentative people is just to agree with them and then wish them a happy day. *"You are absolutely right about that. I'll consider it and how that might fit into my business. Thanks and have a great day."* In their mind, you seem to be agreeing with them, but in actuality you are not. Saying, *"You are right about that,"* is simply an acknowledgement. It is not saying, *"I agree with you and what you are saying, and I will change my business to suit you."* The main thing is to avoid arguing with customers because other customers will feel a negative vibe and leave.

CONCLUSION

With care and some tact, you can learn to handle most situations that arise. Remember not to react too harshly, keep your opinions to yourself, and always behave politely and firmly. This will always serve you well. Try to phrase your responses using the words "and" and "also", instead of "but" or " however". If you say, "thanks for your feedback but I really do have to focus on my customers," what you're really saying is that you are actually not terribly thankful at all for their feedback. If you say, " thanks for your feedback and I do need to focus on my customers," it says that you appreciate their ideas AND you also need to make a living. It's a subtle and powerful distinction that takes some practice. The more you look at conflicts in this way the easier it becomes to allow others their opinions while maintaining your right to a work environment that is focused and enjoyable.

If you are shy and have a difficult time setting boundaries, copy down some of my suggested phrases and practice them in a mirror or with a trusted friend. Act out a scenario and have fun with it, but know that you have a right to a safe and supportive work environment.

As a "captive" audience, it may be difficult to escape some negativity but the way you handle it can either diffuse it or make it worse. In the long run, treating people respectfully and firmly will create a harmonious environment for everyone around you.

Artist Sa Boothroyd in front of her paintings

Pricing and Sales Strategies

An effective pricing strategy makes the difference between average and excellent sales. You want customers to feel that they are receiving good value for their dollar. At the same time you want to make a profit.

PRICING STRATEGIES

Consider the following strategies when pricing your products:

- Avoid undervaluing your product. This contributes to the overall lowering of perceived quality and value in the marketplace. Remember that the choice to forgo proper evaluation of costs affects not only your business, but also damages customer perceptions by keeping prices artificially low. This can actually block serious professionals from making a sustainable living. By selling your own products at prices lower than what is needed to make a real profit, you effectively force other vendors to do the same in order to compete.

- Try to avoid giving discounts. If possible, try to give out free product with a minimum purchase. It gets more products out into the marketplace. This increases your market share and informs more of the public about your products. Simply discounting does not accomplish this at all. Just make sure you work the numbers so that the free product can be expensed on your books as a promotional expense, or the retail price of your other products will compensate for the cost of the free item.

- Limit the number of prices on offer. Keep it simple and limited. Too many choices means that customers have to stand there doing the math, and trying to figure out where they'll save the most money. There is a wonderful video online on one of my favorite websites: www.ted.com   It's called the Paradox of Choice and is well worth watching to expand on this concept. Here is the link.

     http://www.ted.com/talks/lang/eng/barry
     schwartz_on_the_paradox_of_choice.html

- If you sell ten different scone mixes, price them all the same, even if they cost different amounts to make. Calculate the average cost and then mark the product up from there or mark up from the mix that costs you the most.

- Do not create too many *"Buy two, get one free"* type of offers. Offer one or two great deals and that is all. Make certain you can afford to offer product for free.

- If you have one knockout product that sells really well, do not offer deals on it. If it is that good of a seller, you do not need to. That being said, you can always hike up the price of the item, then offer a "discount" if they buy two. This way, you are still getting the price you actually wanted for individual items.

- If you do the *"Buy four, get a free hat"* type of deal, and two friends come up each wanting to buy two items, give them the deal. I would rather sell something than risk losing the sale by being so picky about who gets the deal.

- Sometimes though, customers ask for a discount on only one item. They try to bargain you down. *"If I buy this, will you give me a deal?"* This is not usually acceptable at markets.

- Reward good customers with free product. Record the gift and expense it out as a promotional item. It is easier to keep an existing customer than it is getting new ones. Treat them well, especially if they bring you other customers. It makes them feel special if you offer them something extra and say thank you to them for being such a good customer.

- If you sell by the pound, then never round up prices, always round down. If the cherries weigh in at $4.27, then offer them at $4.25. Better yet, always try to increase the sale. Weigh out a little more than what they wanted and ask if that's ok. They usually say yes, so throw in a couple of extra as a bonus.

- Up selling works really well if you know how to do it. The *"Would you like fries with that?"* strategy really can work, but you have to be creative. When you are selling food, it is always good to have a recipe of the week if you are trying to move a certain product. Tell customers: *"Here's an amazing recipe for the eggplant you've just bought, but you really need this squash and a zucchini for the recipe."* Or *"You really need a few more of those berries for your pie because I guarantee you'll eat half of them before you get home."* If someone is not sure about getting one or getting two, then tell them: *"Well, get two and then you'll have a gift for someone when you need one."* It is a bit cliché to say that, but I'm amazed at how often it works.

- A common pricing strategy in large stores is to price things like, $6.99 or $6.97. There are several psychological reasons for this, but mainly, it is because there are supposedly tipping points where a customer will refuse a product. It is *not* $7.00, it is $6.00 and change. What I do not like about this kind of pricing at the market is that you end up having to keep a lot of change in your float.

- Try to price in round numbers if you can, even if you have to collect taxes. Include the taxes into the price of the product and make sure that your signage clearly informs the customers of your tax obligation. *"Taxes of 15% have been included in the price of all products."* If you do it this way, carefully track each sale and its included tax so you'll know how much to submit to the tax authority. Make sure you can tell your customers exactly how much each product is without the tax. Find out if this is a legal retail practice in your area.

- Have a mix of prices. If you are an artist, bring at least a few of your higher end items to show people the pinnacle of your work, but then have affordable items available, like prints or greeting cards, note pads, playing cards, t-shirts, bags or even puzzles.

- Make use of "frequent buyer" cards. It encourages customer loyalty. Punch cards, stamps, or initials all work and this can be used for almost anything you sell. Offer a free item once they've reached a certain sales amount or number of purchases. Let your customers keep their own cards because it will take too much of your time managing the cards. No card, no stamp.

- Combine deals with other vendors. If you are a potter selling coffee mugs, make a deal with the local coffee roaster that if a customer buys five mugs all at one time, they'll get a coupon for a free pound of coffee. When they pay for the mugs, give them the free coffee coupon and have them redeem it at the coffee vendor. Figure out what you'll pay the coffee vendor and create an agreement that benefits you both.

- Sometimes you are just selling your products too cheaply. Simply raising your prices can result in sales that were not happening before. There can be a powerful change in perception of the value of the products when you increase your prices. Under-priced goods can be interpreted as being of lower quality and less desirable.

Developing effective pricing strategies takes time, experience and experimentation. As you add or discontinue products, pricing will be an ongoing balancing act, so be prepared to change pricing structures as you grow.

Customers understand that prices do increase, but may become annoyed if you make changes too frequently during a season. If you are going to increase pricing, try to do it at the beginning of the season instead of part way through. Take time to accurately cost your products, assign fair prices and then evaluate the response before making any changes.

SALES STRATEGIES

Learning to sell is a skill anyone can learn, but the key is to develop techniques that work for your personality. Certainly try out different techniques that are new to you, but never force your personality into a sales style that is not who you are. If you are shy and reserved, utilizing a high energy, high-pressure sales technique will only serve to drain your energy and create confusion and distrust in your customers. You might be able to sustain the energy of acting like a super salesperson for a while, but it simply cannot last if it is not who you are.

A lot also depends on the characteristics of the people where you live. I live on the west coast of Canada on Vancouver Island, a place known for its casual lifestyle. It sometimes drives me crazy how seemingly laid back and slow the pace of business can be here compared to when I lived in Toronto and Japan. Sales techniques that work in one place may not work in another place. Make careful observations of how people respond to your style and make adjustments accordingly.

Some people are assertive, while others prefer to wait until a customer actually picks something up before speaking to them. If you are shy, selling high demand products will be so much easier for you than selling products that require a sophisticated sales pitch and a lot of customer education.

Whatever your style or personality, there are some concepts to consider if you are looking at making consistent sales at the markets. There is a fairly standard sales cycle that applies in most situations.

Consider the following ideas and ask yourself if you can improve in any of these areas.

1. Attracting the customer's interest.

2. Learning what their needs are and showing how your products will benefit them or solve a problem they may have

3. Closing the sale.

ATTRACTING YOUR CUSTOMER'S INTEREST

- Create an attractive display with effective signs and color schemes.

- Stand up, smile warmly and greet people passing by. Sitting hunched over in a chair reading the paper will only encourage people to keep walking. Why would they want to disturb you?

- Use greetings that bring people into your stall: *"Come feel this baby alpaca wool. It is so soft."* or *"I have something perfect to go with that rhubarb you are carrying."* or *"Come see my new products."* While aggressively hawking or calling out to customers is discouraged at many markets, there is nothing wrong with gently greeting people as they walk by.

- Hand out samples. Do not ask if they want a sample; just get one ready and say: *"Here, try my new chutney!"*

- Mirror behavior. If a customer is quiet and soft, be quiet and soft. If they are loud and boisterous, be loud and boisterous back. If they are touching their hair a lot and leaning forward, do the same. Mirroring makes people feel comfortable and at ease.

- Do not spend your time commenting on their clothes, dogs, accessories, or children. Saying, *"Nice hat, wanna buy some beans?"* is hard to pull off unless you have exceptional charisma, playfulness and can read people well.

- After you've made a sales pitch and the customer is quietly considering a purchase, do not interrupt them by asking them where they bought their coat. It will distract them or remind them that they need to leave to pick up their dry cleaning.

EXPLAINING HOW YOUR PRODUCT CAN BENEFIT THEM

Focus on what you have to offer and how it can benefit your customer. For example, if they have lots of shopping bags with produce, ask them what they are making for dinner, and tie up loose ends for their dinner party by offering them one of your hand woven table runners, your new dessert sauce, pottery for their center piece, or beeswax candles.

Most people who choose to shop at markets are already customers who see the value in shopping locally and have an appreciation for market products. Instead of saying: *"Are you looking for a gift or are you looking for something special?"* just assume they are. When you ask a customer a question, listen carefully to what they are saying. Allow them the time to answer and then explain how one of your products will benefit them.

If someone is looking at your products, ask yourself what their possible needs could be and try to ask questions that will illicit a response that will allow you to positively highlight your products. For example, if a sweaty couple comes into your stall wearing running gear, it is a pretty good bet they are committed to health and fitness. Say something like: *"Athletes really like my muscle rub because it helps reduce muscle inflammation after a run."*

Better yet, if you have a friend who is a competitive athlete, why not get a photo of him holding up your product and have him sign the photo? Or donate product to a local team and display their testimonials.

If it is a person who is in a wheel chair or someone with obvious arthritis, just tailor your statement to them. *"Oh, my grandmother uses these bath salts and they really work well to take away the pain."* Do not lie about it, but make your statements match the person in front of you.

Notice who your main customers are and then make a list of all the issues and challenges they may face. Create a list of how your products address and solve any of these issues so you'll be ready when someone mentions them to you.

HELPING YOUR PURCHASER DECIDE TO BUY

Various sales techniques can make your products highly desirable. See what works best for you.

Some vendors with lively, funny and assertive manners will simply challenge customers to buy product and it sure can work. *"What, how many shirts do you need to try on? Pick one already!"* Only you can be the judge of whether you can pull off a phrase like that.

Sometimes a regular customer will come by and say they already have one of your items or still have a supply of your products. This is a perfect opportunity to ask them some questions within earshot of new customers:

- *"Oh yes, you bought my beautiful blue sweater last week. What are you wearing with it?"*

- *"Great, what are you using my spice mix on?"*

- *"How are you enjoying my new coffee blend?"*

Happy customers are usually very willing to tell you about their experiences with your products. It shows other customers that there are, indeed, people who buy and enjoy your products. Just because a regular customer does not need your products one week does not mean you should not talk to them! In fact, you simply cannot pay for such great publicity.

MENTIONING PRODUCT SCARCITY

This is a common technique to encourage sales of a product because of a perception of the product's rarity. At many markets around the world, produce is picked at its perfect ripeness and sometimes the harvest for that item may last only a very short time. This is certainly true for my local asparagus, which is only available for the month of May. Because of the continual availability of imported foods, customers are often conditioned to expect a product to be available at all times of the year.

If you are selling a local product that has a short harvest time, then make sure you heavily advertise that fact in your stall. Put up signs that say: "FINALLY! IT IS ASPARAGUS SEASON, 30 DAYS AND COUNTING!" Remind customers every week what's in season. If it is almost the end of the season, put up another sign: "THE END IS NEAR!" and watch as people come into your stall asking: *"What do you mean, the end is near?"*

It is evocative, and depending on your character, can be quite funny. Still, the whole point is to get customers to understand the limited availability of local goods, especially fresh foods.

OVERCOMING HIDDEN FEARS AND OBJECTIONS

Customers sometimes say: "I buy this stuff and never know how to use it once I get it home." What is the fear behind this statement?" There are several actually. The customer may be thinking, "I will look stupid in front of my family for not knowing what to do with this because I'm not a confident cook." "I would be wasting money buying something I do not know how to use and will get in trouble with my spouse."

What is the solution? Provide flyers that explain how to use your products. If you make beautiful scarves then give them a nice flyer that shows five ways of wearing it. If you are selling eco-friendly cleaning products, provide a flyer that outlines how you are helping the environment and your family's health by using them. Make suggestions for all the things they can clean using your product. Provide easy recipes with photos of dishes made from your ingredients and provide lots of serving suggestions.

The more instructions, recipes, and suggestions you give in a concrete format like a brochure, the more confident customers will feel in buying your product.

OFFERING GUARANTEES

Some people are afraid that family members or friends will not like what they buy from you. Try to offer them a guarantee that if they do not like it, they can bring it back for an exchange or refund within a given time period. Make sure your policies are clearly posted, and on your sales receipts.

HELPING THE HESITANT CUSTOMER

If a customer hesitates to the point of simply stalling, move on to another customer. If they are blocking the front of your stall, you can quite easily just start talking to someone new. You can even ask them to step to one side so you can help someone else while they are deciding. Tell them that exactly: *"Can I ask you to step to the side while you are making your decision so I can help this customer?"* Do you notice that I still inject the idea that they are in the process of making a decision?

I did not say: *"Can you step aside?"* That basically implies that I'm not expecting any sale at all, so why should they buy? They usually snap out of it and realize they are taking up space.

By helping other customers who know exactly what they want, the person hesitating may very well be inspired to buy. If not, they'll walk away and leave you to help other people.

CLOSING THE SALE

If the customer has had all the samples they need, have tried on ten pairs of earrings and are still standing there trying to decide what to buy, it may be time to give them a nudge and close the sale. This is a skill many vendors feel really shy about doing, but there are gentle ways of handling this.

Try some of these phrases:

- "Here, let me wrap that up for you while you continue looking around."

- "Go ahead and put that in your bag if you are done shopping."

- "Do you need a bag to put that in or did you bring your own?"

- "So, who are you cooking my carrots for this evening?"

- "Is there anything else you need before I tally this up?"

- "Oh, by the way, I take cash, or credit and debit cards if you are low on cash."

- "I'd love to get a photo of you wearing my hat at the wedding."

- "Ok, so did you want to take that then?"

- "No, sorry, I do not hold product because it sells too fast. If you want to pay for it now and leave it here while you look around the market, I can put it aside with your name and number on it."

- *"I think you should buy that now because I'm running low and may sell out before you get a chance to come back."* (Only say this if it is true!)

- "If you really like that one you may want to get it now because it is one of a kind and I will not be making any more of that variety."

- "This is the last day for strawberries; get them now or it'll be too late."

I've heard all of these phrases at various times and have used many of them myself. Only the last five suggestions are even remotely pushy, but can easily result in a sale if you say it in a friendly, non-aggressive manner. It will really depend on your personality or style.

CONCLUSION

Keep your pricing simple and do not offer deals unless they work in your favor. Encourage your customers, alleviate their concerns, and if you get a sense that they are open to it, have fun, smile and try out a few of the phrases I've suggested.

Overall, keep focused on your customers' needs and the benefits your products will have in their lives. Soon you will find a rhythm and style that suits who you are.

Dana's Top Ten Lists

$\mathcal{I}$have a few useful top ten lists. In a nutshell, they'll give you an overview of everything you need to know about markets.

TOP TEN SUGGESTIONS FOR A SUCCESSFUL MARKET EXPERIENCE

- Pick a product that has a good chance of selling well in your area.

- Design a beautiful stall and effective signage.

- Save money on packaging and splurge on excellent graphic design.

- Get the help of business professionals as needed.

- Buy supplies at wholesale prices, manufacture efficiently and buy in bulk to reduce costs.

- Develop and practice a good sales pitch.

- Use effective pricing and incentive structures.

- Focus on excellent service and offer good value.

- Keep yourself in good shape, mentally, physically and spiritually.

- Sell, sell sell!

TOP TEN THINGS VENDORS LOVE ABOUT BEING AT THE MARKETS

- It is outside! Fresh air!

- Companionship. Friendships and harmonious working relationships with other vendors can be very gratifying.

- Sense of control over your own destiny. No bosses holding your job ransom.

- Getting a thrill every time someone buys something from you.

- Watching micro-economies at work. There is nothing like seeing money circulate around a market, knowing that this money is not being funneled out of your community into the hands of faceless, corporate giants.

- Counting up a big wad of cash at the end of the day.

- Being able to sell what you want, developing your art, be it the art of raising chickens or sewing a beautiful dress.

- Watching your business grow and feeling the satisfaction of developing a regular clientele.

- Knowing that you are right in the midst of a wave of interest in markets. It is the perfect time to get involved and take control of your life.

- A sense of freedom and community.

TOP TEN THINGS CUSTOMERS LOVE ABOUT BEING AT THE MARKETS

- Access to fresh local food, often organic.

- Enjoyment of locally made, high quality crafts.

- Knowing that the meat they buy was raised ethically by people who care about animal welfare.

- A sense of community spirit.

- Knowing and trusting the people who made what they've bought.

- Enjoying being outside and visiting with friends in the community.

- Knowing that their hard earned money is staying in the community.

- Being proud to show around out-of-town visitors

- Eating that first strawberry or heirloom tomato, right out of the box.

- A quiet sense of freedom and strength they get from living and shopping closer to home.

CONCLUSION

This book has changed a lot since I started writing it and the longer I kept tweaking, the more it reflected the woman I am today. Still, at some point, I had to let go and allow this creation to find its way into your hands, knowing in many ways that it is a work in progress. This can be said of products you create for the market. A market business, like life, grows, changes, and evolves over time. By cultivating a gentle, open heart, you can take an honest look at your business and make the changes that best work for your customers while remaining true to your vision.

Market businesses allow your creativity to flow, and a freedom of expression that may not be available to you in a formal working environment. It is honest and real in a way that lets you know directly when you are the one who makes things happen or let's things slide. You also get first hand experience in what drives a market, what entices customers to buy and then come back week after week to the same stalls. It's a truly amazing experience and one that needs to continue to happen in our world so that we start to reconnect with one another in truthful, healthy, loving and sustainable ways.

A market business isn't a one- stop fix for our world's woes. What it does allow is for us to focus in on the things that we can control, namely, where and from whom we shop. A market brings our world back to a place of simplicity and accountability. It is a place where we know exactly what is happening close to home, a place where we feed and even clothe one another, where we rely on one another, greet each other by name and help nurture the local economy.

I love market life. I love knowing that it's totally up to me whether or not I have a job to go to each day. I love knowing that what I have made is of value and that people come back to me and tell me how they use my products and enjoy them. I embrace the challenges and rewards equally and the difficult times are worth the effort when the result is a life lived with purpose, creativity and inspiration.

From the whole of my heart, I thank you for reading this book and I sincerely hope that it has made the spark of inspiration you hold stronger with the words, " I can do this!"

See you at the market.

Knitted wrist warmers

Bibliography

Branfman, Steven, 1999. *The Potter's Professional Handbook*, Iowa, WI: Kraus Publications.

Clark, Donald A., 2006. *Making a Living in Crafts. Everything You Need to Know to Build a Business.* New York: Lark Books.

Coleman, Eliot, 2009. *The Winter Harvest Handbook.* White River Junction, VT: Chelsea Green Publishing.

Ivanko, John and Lisa Kivirist, 2008. *ECOpreneuring.* Gabriola Island BC: New Society Publishers.

Kadubec, Philip, 2007. *Crafts and Craft Shows. How to Make Money.* 2nd ed. New York: Allworth Press.

Laurie, Jo and Steven Fenton, 2007. *Craft in America. Celebrating Two Centuries of Artists and Objects.* New York: Clarkson Potter Publishers.

Ramsey, Dan, 1997. *The Crafter's Guide to Pricing Your Work. How to Calculate the Value of Your Time, Materials and Handiwork to Make Money with Your Crafts.* Ohio: Betterway Books.

Wasinger, Susan, 2009. *Eco Craft.* New York: Lark Books.

photo by Sarah Hall

About the Author

$\mathcal{S}$ince 2004, Dana Zaruba has been manufacturing and selling her own line of gourmet food products under the name Hot Chick Spice Company. With a Bachelor of Applied Arts in Production Management, an MA in Counseling Psychology and years of teaching English as a Second Language, she has used her education to effectively shape her business as a reflection of her values and creative interests.

Dana continues to sell through farmers' markets, festivals, Christmas craft fairs and also maintains a small wholesale business. Dana strives to keep life simple and balanced and realizes that keeping her business small allows her the time and freedom to also pursue her other loves of painting, cooking and reading.

She is also an award nominee in the food and beverage category by Mid Island Science and Technology Innovation Council (MISTIC) and plans on launching a series of hands on workshops to expand on the themes presented in this book.

Coming soon. . .

Learn from Dana Zaruba herself as she hosts a series of online and in person workshops to teach people how to run successful market stalls. Please visit her website or send her an e-mail for more information.

Website: www.overunitypress.com
E-mail: danazaruba@overunitypress.com